Cliffs
Getting a Job

By Carol Kleiman

IN THIS BOOK

- Analyze your career goals and objectives
- Discover your ideal career
- Find out what you need to know to conduct a job search
- Create an attention-getting resume and cover letter
- Ace the job interview
- Reinforce what you learn with CliffsNotes Review
- Find more information about getting a job in CliffsNotes Resource Center and online at www.cliffsnotes.com

IDG Books Worldwide, Inc.
An International Data Group Company
Foster City, CA • Chicago, IL • Indianapolis, IN • New York, NY

About the Author

Carol Kleiman, nationally syndicated Jobs columnist for the *Chicago Tribune*, is the prize-winning author of *The 100 Best Jobs for the 1990s and Beyond* and *The Career Coach*.

Publisher's Acknowledgments

Editorial

Project Editor: Kelly Ewing

Acquisitions Editor: Karen Hansen

Technical Editor(s): Perri Capell

Production

Indexer: York Production Services, Inc.

Proofreader: York Production Services, Inc.

IDG Books Indianapolis Production Department

CliffsNotes™ Getting a Job

Published by

IDG Books Worldwide, Inc.

An International Data Group Company

919 E. Hillsdale Blvd.

Suite 400

Foster City, CA 94404

www.idgbooks.com (IDG Books Worldwide Web site)

www.cliffsnotes.com (CliffsNotes Web site)

Library of Congress Catalog Card No.: 99-67260

ISBN: 0-7645-8535-5

Printed in the United States of America

10 9 8 7 6 5 4 3 2 1

1O/RQ/RS/ZZ/IN

Distributed in the United States by IDG Books Worldwide, Inc.

Distributed by CDG Books Canada Inc. for Canada; by Transworld Publishers Limited in the United Kingdom; by IDG Norge Books for Norway; by IDG Sweden Books for Sweden; by IDG Books Australia Publishing Corporation Pty. Ltd. for Australia and New Zealand; by TransQuest Publishers Pte Ltd. for Singapore, Malaysia, Thailand, Indonesia, and Hong Kong; by Gotop Information Inc. for Taiwan; by ICG Muse, Inc. for Japan; by Intersoft for South Africa; by Eyrolles for France; by International Thomson Publishing for Germany, Austria and Switzerland; by Distribuidora Cuspide for Argentina; by LR International for Brazil; by Galileo Libros for Chile; by Ediciones ZETA S.C.R. Ltda. for Peru; by WS Computer Publishing Corporation, Inc., for the Philippines; by Contemporanea de Ediciones for Venezuela; by Express Computer Distributors for the Caribbean and West Indies; by Micronesia Media Distributor, Inc. for Micronesia; by Chips Computadoras S.A. de C.V. for Mexico; by Editorial Norma de Panama S.A. for Panama; by American Bookshops for Finland.

For general information on IDG Books Worldwide's books in the U.S., please call our Consumer Customer Service department at **800-762-2974.** For reseller information, including discounts and premium sales, please call our Reseller Customer Service department at **800-434-3422.**

For information on where to purchase IDG Books Worldwide's books outside the U.S., please contact our International Sales department at 317-596-5530 or fax **317-596-5692.**

For consumer information on foreign language translations, please contact our Customer Service department at **1-800-434-3422,** fax 317-596-5692, or e-mail rights@idgbooks.com.

For information on licensing foreign or domestic rights, please phone **+1-650-655-3109.**

For sales inquiries and special prices for bulk quantities, please contact our Sales department at 650-655-3200 or write to the address above.

For information on using IDG Books Worldwide's books in the classroom or for ordering examination copies, please contact our Educational Sales department at **800-434-2086** or fax 317-596-5499.

For press review copies, author interviews, or other publicity information, please contact our Public Relations department at **650-655-3000** or fax **650-655-3299.**

For authorization to photocopy items for corporate, personal, or educational use, please contact Copyright Clearance Center, 222 Rosewood Drive, Danvers, MA 01923, or fax **978-750-4470.**

Table of Contents

Introduction 1

Why Do You Need This Book? 1

How to Use This Book 2

Don't Miss Our Web Site 3

Chapter 1: Focusing on Your Goals and Career Choices 5

Determining Your Wants and Needs 6

Assessing your situation 6

Creating your five-year plan 8

Getting Help 10

Consulting with career counselors 10

Visiting career placement centers 11

Consulting with retail career marketers 11

Utilizing outplacement services 12

Comparing types of job search help 12

Switching Careers 13

Focusing on your transferable skills 13

Knowing what employers want 14

Honing your communication skills 15

Finding a Job You Enjoy 16

Matching preferences to jobs 16

Narrowing your choices 18

Chapter 2: Matching Your Goals to Today's Job Market 19

Finding a Job You Enjoy in a Growing Field .19

Recognizing the hottest fields 20

Moving away from fields that are not growing 28

Gathering Information about a Job 29

Informational interviewing 29

Job shadowing 30

Volunteering 31

Working on internships 31

Chapter 3: Doing Your Homework 33

Doing Your Homework 33

Basic questions to ask 34

Compatibility questions to ask 35

Finding the Answers 36
  Using the Internet 36
  Using the library 38
  Using the media 39

Chapter 4: The Job Search 41
Beginning Your Search 41
  Using classified ads 42
  Using the telephone 42
  Using the Internet 43
  Using your college's resources 45
Joining Professional Organizations 45
  Using job banks 46
  Getting the word out at meetings 46
Trying Other Methods 47
  Job clubs 47
  Job fairs 48
  Headhunters 49
  Employment agencies, temporary services, and part-time work 50
  Networking 52

Chapter 5: Creating Your Ticket to Success: The Resume 53
To Reveal or Not to Reveal 54
  Personal items you don't want to mention 54
  What about volunteer work? 55
  What about why I'm job hunting? 55
  What about salaries? 55
Understanding the Three Types of Resumes 56
  The chronological resume (the one employers want most) 57
  The skills or functional resume 57
  The historical or anecdotal resume 60

**Chapter 6: Packaging Yourself: The Cover Letter and
Resume Presentation 65**
What a Cover Letter Can Do for You 65
  What a good cover letter does for you 66
  What to leave out of the cover letter 67
Creating the Cover Letter 67
  Cover letter for the chronological resume 68
  Cover letter for the skills (or functional) resume 68
  Cover letter for the historical (or anecdotal) resume 68

Modifying Your Cover Letter 72
Submitting Your Cover Letter and Resume 72
   Delivering your cover letter and resume in person 73
   Mailing your cover letter and resume 73
   Faxing your cover letter and resume 74
   E-mailing your cover letter and resume 74
   Posting your resume on the Internet 75
Following Up 76

Chapter 7: Gathering References: Your Job Insurance **77**
Compiling Your References 77
   Securing the best references 78
   Gathering references 79
   Fighting a bad reference 82
Keeping in Touch with Your References 83

Chapter 8: The Job Interview **84**
Arranging the Interview 84
Selling Yourself 85
   Questions you'll be asked 86
   Acing written tests 88
   Questions you shouldn't answer 89
Asking the Right Questions 90
   Business-related questions 90
   Work life versus personal life questions 91
Standing out in a Crowd 92
   How to end the interview 92
   Don't forget to write a thank you 92
   Warn your references 93
That All-Important Second Interview (and Third, and Fourth . . .) 93
   Getting a second interview 93
   Changing your focus 95
   Fitting in with the company culture 95
   Following up 96

Chapter 9: Nailing the Job **97**
Keeping in Touch 97
The Job Offer 98
   Doing your salary homework 98
   Discussing the salary with confidence 99
   Negotiating your salary 99

Ways to increase your offer 100
Negotiating benefits 101
Special considerations 102
Accepting the Job Offer 102
Get it in writing 102
Signing contracts 103

Chapter 10: Life After the Job **105**
Giving Notice 105
Leaving immediately 106
Staying on 106
Getting through the Last Two Weeks 107
Handling the exit interview 107
Cleaning up the odds and ends 108
Hitting the Ground Running 108
Organizing your work life 108
Acing your first day 109

CliffsNotes Review **111**
Q&A 111
Scenario 112
Consider This 112
Practice Project 113

CliffsNotes Resource Center **114**
Books 114
Internet 115
Send Us Your Favorite Tips 116

Index **117**

INTRODUCTION

Getting a job takes a lot of work, and every job seeker needs up-to-date information and step-by-step suggestions on how to proceed. Whether you're applying for your first job, changing jobs, or switching careers, you must have current data on today's employment market and expert advice in order to be competitive. Conducting a job search is a serious challenge, but this book unmasks the secrets of a successful search by clearly explaining where the jobs are, how to apply for them, and how to get them.

Unfortunately, many job seekers think that all they have to do is send a resume, but that's not enough to land a position in a labor market where the best jobs are avidly sought after. Instead, a lot of preparation is involved, and this book helps you get ready for the task of finding the opening you want — one in your field with a good salary, good benefits, and a clear career path.

Why Do You Need This Book?

Can you answer yes to any of these questions?

- Do you need to find out how to get a job fast?
- Are you too busy to read 500 pages on how to get a job?
- Do you want to know how to complete a self-assessment and find jobs that match your abilities and interests?
- Do you want to find out which jobs are hottest in today's economy and the requirements to qualify for them?
- Do you need help creating your resume, your ticket to success?

If so, then CliffsNotes *Getting a Job* is for you!

How to Use This Book

You're the boss here. You get to decide how to read this book. You can review it from cover to cover or seek only the information you want and put it back on the shelf for later. However, I'll tell you about a few ways I recommend to find your topics.

- Use the index in the back of the book to find what you're looking for.

- Flip through the book, looking for your topic in the running heads.

- Look for your topic in the Table of Contents in the front of the book.

- Look at the In This Chapter list at the beginning of each chapter.

- Look for additional information in the Resource Center or test your knowledge in the Review section.

- Flip through the book until you find what you're looking for — I organized the book in a logical, task-oriented way.

Also, to find important information quickly, you can look for icons strategically placed in the text. Here is a description of the icons you'll find in this book:

If you see a Remember icon, make a mental note of this text — it's worth keeping in mind.

If you see a Tip icon, you'll know that you've run across a helpful hint, uncovered a secret, or received good advice.

The Warning icon alerts you to something that could be dangerous, requires special caution, or should be avoided.

Don't Miss Our Web Site

Keep up with the changing world of getting a job by visiting the CliffsNotes Web site at www.cliffsnotes.com. Here's what you find:

- Interactive tools that are fun and informative
- Links to interesting Web sites
- Additional resources to help you continue your learning

At www.cliffsnotes.com, you can even register for a new feature called CliffsNotes Daily, which offers you newsletters on a variety of topics, delivered right to your e-mail inbox each business day.

If you haven't yet discovered the Internet and are wondering how to get online, pick up *Getting On the Internet*, new from CliffsNotes. You'll learn just what you need to make your online connection quickly and easily. See you at www.cliffsnotes.com!

CHAPTER 1

FOCUSING ON YOUR GOALS AND CAREER CHOICES

IN THIS CHAPTER

- Determining your professional wants and needs

- Setting your personal and professional goals for the next five years

- Finding out which (if any) career service is appropriate for your job search

- Understanding what's involved in planning a career change

- Seeing how your specific interests tie into your career options

Finding the job that's right for you begins with choosing a career, field, or profession — one that matches your qualifications, that has the potential to allow you to move up the career ladder, and that will make you happy. And the way you find the job that's best for you is by analyzing what it is you want to do and how you want to live your life.

Now is the time to sit down and do some deep soul-searching and serious research on yourself to evaluate where you want to spend at least eight hours a day, five days a week, for many years to come. Even if you're looking for another job in the same profession you're in now, it's still a good idea to begin with an honest self-evaluation.

Determining Your Wants and Needs

You probably already know what it is you like to do — and it's usually what you do best. Write down your skills, achievements, passions, and goals. What are your weaknesses, ? What do you absolutely hate doing? What do you love?

If you're a first-time job seeker, what are you prepared for professionally? What really holds your interest? If you're a job changer, evaluate the drawbacks of your current position, the reasons you want to leave, in order to avoid repeating them. Then list the advantages, in order to duplicate them in a new position.

If you're changing careers, assess what attracts you to your new field and compare your findings to what you disliked in your previous profession. You want to avoid repeating the same disappointments and frustrations.

Assessing your situation

Here are ten questions you should ask yourself — and answer. They give you needed insight into what really matters to you. Later in this chapter, your answers can help you choose a career or a job that is likely to provide most of the things that you value.

- Do you enjoy working with numbers?

- Do computers fascinate you?

- Does production and assembly work interest you?

- Is an excellent salary your No. 1 priority?

- Do you prefer close supervision, or do you prefer to be left on your own to get the job done?

- Is helping others one of your career goals?

- Does working directly with the public appeal to you?

- Are you a team player?

- Do you prefer working on short-term projects rather than long-term assignments?

- Do you like problem-solving?

- Does managing others appeal to you?

Be completely honest in evaluating what you're looking for in a job and in your life. If you're not truthful, the only person you'll be fooling is yourself. And the only time you'll be wasting in your job hunt will be your own.

In order to find out what it is you want to do and what personal satisfactions you need to achieve the lifestyle you desire, you also need to rate the importance of the following factors.

Scale of 10

- Medical insurance *8*

- Dental insurance *8*

- Vision care *8*

- Other medical coverage *4*

- Starting salary *7*

- Opportunities for advancement *10*

- Working conditions *6*

- Flexible work hours *6*

- Friendly colleagues *8*

- Understanding managers *8*

- Good company culture and ethics *9*

- Training programs *8*

- Travel opportunities *3*

- Family-friendly benefits, such as child care *2*

- Incentive compensation *5*

After you've analyzed the job characteristics that you're looking for, the next step is an assessment of yourself and what you need to feel satisfied, to wake up each morning eager to go to work. You should ask yourself the following questions.

■ How important are recognition, frequent pats on the back, and visibility to you?

■ Does where you work, the actual physical environment, matter?

■ Do you feel it's important to be informed about what's going on in the entire organization, not just your department?

■ Do you want frequent discussions with your manager about your career goals, input from supervisors, and feedback on your job performance?

■ Do you want to work for an employer who offers continuing training, both formal and informal?

■ Are you looking for an organization that is supportive of your need to balance your work, family, and personal lives and responsibilities?

Don't expect to find a job that meets all your requirements — even if you start your own business. But it is possible to find one that meets most of them, which is what you want to aim for.

Creating your five-year plan

When you have a handle on what really matters to you — remember that typically you'll spend more hours working than doing anything else over your lifetime — draw up a five-year plan of where you are going and how you expect to get there. Your projection of where you hope your needs, values, and skills will lead you also will help steer you to the job, career, or profession that you are best suited for. Some people create two plans, one that seems realistic and achievable, the other a fantasy. While I acknowledge the importance of having a dream — everyone should have one — I encourage you first to find an achievable one. You can dream after you get the job you're looking for.

Here are suggested ingredients for your realistic five-year plan. List your answers year by year.

- Where do you want to be professionally each year for the next five years? Give job title or promotion you hope to achieve each year.

- How much money do you expect to make?

- What size company do you want to work for?

- What responsibilities do you expect to be given?

- What skills do you want to learn from your job?

- What additional education, such as courses, training, language skill, or degrees, do you hope to acquire?

- What professional organizations do you want to join, and what role will you play in them?

- What are your plans, year by year, for marriage, family, and relationships?

- How will you spend your leisure time? Plot your plans for such activities as travel, sports, recreation, friends, and volunteer and community work.

- What kind of lifestyle is your goal? Include geographical location, cultural advantages, city or suburban life, having fun, income level, and type of home that you want.

Organize your five-year plan into one-year segments — and also include where you hope to be in your personal life. Write down each year of the next five years and put your goals — realistic ones — under each year.

Five-year plans are not written in stone. Don't feel that by designing one you'll be locking yourself into an agenda that may be too difficult for you.

A five-year plan is a road map: It's not the exact trip you'll be taking. Instead, it's a guide and a measure along the way of every step in finding the job that's best for you and succeeding in your career.

Getting Help

Some job seekers need more help in evaluating their skills and in drawing up plans. Even though I think you know better than anyone else what you want to do and I don't think anyone should rely completely on a standardized test, psychological testing often is a very helpful launching pad for job seekers. One of the most frequently used tests is the Myers-Briggs Type Indicator, which will give you additional insight into the profession that's most compatible with your personality. This instrument helps you identify your specific personality type, so you know what kinds of jobs you're suited for.

Psychologists and psychological testing usually offer valuable insight into which career is best for you and help build your confidence.

Consulting with career counselors

Another professional available to help guide you is a private career counselor who also will test you and give hands-on advice on how to achieve your goals. Not every state requires career counselors to be licensed, so almost anyone can hang out a shingle. When shopping for a career counselor, ask for credentials, references, and details such as how many sessions you will need and fees. For a referral to a certified career counselor in your geographical area, call the National Board for Certified Counselors at 336-547-0607.

Visiting career placement centers

If you can't afford private counseling, contact the career counseling center of your local college. Their staffs are qualified, and their fees usually are lower than those of private career consultants. Another good source of counseling is your college placement center. They also are abreast of demand in the job market because of their contacts with recruiters visiting campus and the many job openings they receive from employers. Services usually are free for current students and alumni.

Consulting with retail career marketers

Career marketers also help prepare job seekers for their job search, but you have to be wary of them. Many of them charge thousands of dollars up front. They talk about connecting clients to the "hidden job market," but for many dissatisfied clients, that market remains "hidden." Many of the complaints I get about career marketers is that they promise you jobs but don't get you one. Career marketers say that they don't guarantee that clients will find new jobs — just that they'll receive help with the techniques needed to secure new positions. Before signing on with a career marketing firm, check it out with the Better Business Bureau and your state attorney general's office. Ask for references from previous clients.

Try to avoid paying a large sum of money in advance of any professional career counseling service you receive. Instead, only pay for each stage of the help you receive as you get it.

Utilizing outplacement services

If you've been downsized or a victim of a layoff and your company offers you outplacement services, take it! Outplacement counselors, like other career counselors, do not get you a job, but they do a very effective job of helping you analyze and weaknesses and rebuild your confidence. Another positive: Your former employer pays the bill, not you.

Comparing types of job search help

The following list shows you the advantages and disadvantages of the different types of job search help available.

- **Career counselors:** Pros: Administer tests. Gives you hands-on, personalized advice. Cons: May not be licensed or qualified. Suggested action: Ask potential career counselors for credentials, references, and fees. Call the National Board for Certified Counselors at 336-547-0607 for a licensed career counselor in your area.

- **Career placement centers:** Pros: Usually less expensive than a private career counselor. Often free for currently enrolled students and alumni. Easy to find because most colleges offer this service, including your alma mater. Have connections with many businesses and nonprofit organizations looking to fill positions. Suggested action: Contact your college to ask about career counseling and any costs involved. Or call a local college's career center and ask whether staff would be willing to help you for a fee. Look in the local phone book for nearby community colleges and ask them if they have a career placement center and if you can use it.

- **Career marketers:** Pros: Administer tests. Hands-on, personalized advice. May be well connected with business and nonprofit organizations looking to fill positions. Cons: Can be very expensive and require payment before services are rendered. May promise you a job in a hidden market only they are privy to, but never actually find you a job. Suggested action: Check them out with the Better Business Bureau or your state's attorney's office. Ask for credentials, references, and fees.

- **Outplacement services:** Pros: Free — the company laying you off pays for this service. Help you analyze and weaknesses and rebuild your confidence.

Switching Careers

If you're switching not only jobs but careers, it's essential to talk to professionals in your new field, to academic deans, and to heads of departments and to do your homework on the future of the career you're switching to before you make your move. You may need additional educational courses or degrees. You may find your new choice isn't a growing profession. It may turn out not to suit you temperamentally. And, you probably will have to take a decrease in salary.

Focusing on your transferable skills

When changing careers, be aware of the skills you now have, which ones are transferable to your new field and the new ones you will acquire in your new job. One advantage of changing careers in a highly volatile economy is the opportunity to add new skills to your portfolio to make you more marketable for your next job. It's an important consideration in career changing.

Tip

You're to be congratulated for leaving a field you don't like and entering one you really care about. But give yourself enough time before making the switch to make sure that you're qualified and prepared in every way to succeed in it.

Knowing what employers want

Whether you're looking for a job, transferring internally, or pursuing a new career, keep in mind that someone has to hire you. That's why savvy job seekers ask, "What do employers want?" The right answers will help you decide where you best fit in and will be pivotal in directing your job search.

All employers want to hire people with the skills the company needs, though many companies will do some initial training if they really want you on board. This is particularly true today in high-tech jobs: Because of the scarcity of skilled technical professionals, more and more high-tech companies, particularly those in Silicon Valley, are willing to hire so-called "low-tech" job applicants and train them to work at higher levels.

Your current skills may get you in the door for a job interview, but other factors determine whether you get a job offer.

Most employers want people who have a good work ethic, who rarely are absent, and who always are on time. After these basics are satisfied, employers look for workers who are

- Team players
- Flexible
- Adaptable
- Open to ongoing training
- Compatible with colleagues

- A problem-solver

- Highly motivated

- Positive — not negative — attitude

- Good communication skills

- Able to identify problems and solve them

Just as you work to acquire professional skills, you also can work at developing the personality characteristics that employers want and need.

Honing your communication skills

In an information society, one of the most important traits a job seeker needs is excellent communication skills. You have to be able to articulate your thoughts and to speak well — it's as simple as that. And to speak up. Strong verbal skills are your best bet to explain what you can do and to sell yourself to a prospective employer. Then, once you're on the job, you need good communication skills to get the work done, especially in an employment situation where the emphasis is on teamwork.

Good communication skills also involve listening to and understanding what's being said and giving others a chance to speak.

If you're concerned about how you communicate, improve your speaking skills by taking group speech classes or going to a speech therapist for help. Check the yellow pages for professionals in the field or call your local community college or university for names.

Finding a Job You Enjoy

Finding a job you enjoy leads not only to professional but personal satisfaction as well: You'll spend most of your waking hours working. And doing what you like creates confidence and a sense of power. Passion for the task at hand is empowering and exciting. With the long hours demanded by most employers, enjoying what you're doing, respecting your coworkers and your managers, achieving your goals, empowering other people, and serving a real need make the tough road of work easier to travel.

Don't blindly accept a job, even one that seems right to you, without asking questions about the corporate culture and what it's like to work at the company on a daily basis.

Matching preferences to jobs

Earlier in this chapter, I listed important questions you should ask yourself to help determine what fields you may be best suited for and what job might make you happy. The following list shows you the characteristics you examined and some of the jobs they dovetail with.

- If you enjoy working with numbers, try the following jobs: accountant, investment analyst, banker, math teacher, statistician, technician, scientist, or retail clerk.

- If you are fascinated by computers, try the following jobs: Web master, program analyst, graphic artist, systems analyst, computer equipment operator, network specialist, researcher, or electronic media reporter or editor.

- If you find production and assembly work appealing, try the following jobs: mechanic, machinist, project manager, repairer, installer, construction worker, production supervisor, or desktop publisher.

■ If your main goal is to make a lot of money, try the following jobs: financial services executive, doctor, lawyer, stockbroker, television anchor, entertainer, professional athlete, systems programmer, computer analyst, real estate developer, or executive chef.

■ If you know you need close supervision, try the following jobs: nursing aide, laboratory assistant, bank employee, security guard, technician, metal worker, production worker, waiter or waitress, private household worker, or heavy equipment operator.

■ If you prefer to work on your own, try the following jobs: engineer, journalist, bartender, bookkeeper, nurse practitioner, cosmetologist, carpenter, scientist, doctor, lawyer, dentist, veterinarian, designer, or air traffic controller.

■ If you want to help others, try the following jobs: healthcare worker, social worker, teacher, publisher, architect, psychologist, geriatric specialist, child care provider, athletic coach, police officer, firefighter, government worker, or educational administrator.

■ If you enjoy working with the public, try the following jobs: salesperson, transportation worker, cashier, hotel worker, human resources personnel, healthcare worker, librarian, public relations consultant, real estate agent, telemarketer, waiter or waitress, flight attendant, travel agent, community organizer, or local, state, or federal official.

■ If you have strong communication skills, try the following jobs: radio or television broadcaster, journalist, entertainer, salesperson, supervisor, manager, teacher, administrator, medical technician, agent, business consultant, counselor, or advertising and marketing executive

- If you're a team player, try the following jobs: manufacturing and production worker, actor, musician, computer programmer, clerk, administrative assistant, technical writer, dispatcher, agricultural worker, zookeeper, or corporate employee.

- If you prefer short-term projects, try the following jobs: computer technician, dental technician, repairer, mechanic, electrician, photographer, news reporter, truck driver, job trainer, welding machine operator, or optician insurance adjuster.

Narrowing your choices

You probably will find that a variety of jobs and professions interest you. Carefully narrow them down to fit your personality traits and skills.

Now that you have a handle on your interests and skills and some of the jobs they fit with, you're ready to learn which jobs have the most growth potential and the qualifications for them. In Chapter 2, you'll find the top fields of employment and the growth jobs in them.

CHAPTER 2

MATCHING YOUR GOALS TO TODAY'S JOB MARKET

IN THIS CHAPTER

- Finding a job you enjoy in a growing field
- Discovering the qualifications for the hottest jobs
- Figuring out the best way to learn about the job you want

Before you begin job hunting, you should choose the field that's best for you — one that offers a promising future, opportunity, and an abundance of jobs — and that best fits your skills. If you choose a career with good prospects, you have purchased employment insurance for yourself and reduced the chance of finding yourself stuck in a dead-end job.

There still are some good jobs in declining fields such as mining or manufacturing, and if these fields are where your passion lies, don't rule them out. But if you have the choice, it makes much more sense to focus your job search in a profession that's expanding and will be around for several decades.

Finding a Job You Enjoy in a Growing Field

Finding a job in an area that is projected to grow significantly over the next decade is a smart career move. The United States' economy, previously known as an industrial society and before that described as an agricultural one, now is an information and high-tech economy, which means service jobs are the ones most plentiful. The service-production sector is the area where services, rather than goods, are created. It includes such fields as business, health care, legal, educational, personal, and social services. Other divisions include government, utilities, sales, transportation, communications, travel, finance, insurance, real estate, and travel.

Not every position in the service-producing sector is growing. Accountants, for example, are in demand, but auditing clerks are not. Figure 2-1 gives you the scoop on the demand in each field.

Recognizing the hottest fields

Though there are millions of jobs in the *goods-producing sector* of the economy — the industrial division of the U.S. economy that includes the manufacture of durable and nondurable goods — the greatest job growth in the next decade is expected to occur in the services sector.

Wholesale trade, transportation, construction, mining, and agriculture — often calculated separately by the bureau — accounted for the rest of the job growth.

Service positions are expected to claim an even larger share of the job market. At the same time, the share of jobs in manufacturing is expected to diminish.

Today, the hottest area, the one with the greatest and fastest job growth, is information technology. Anything connected with computers, except for computer operators who input data, will be a good job with a good future. So if you're fascinated by technology, you're well suited to break into this field.

Next in order of growth are business and financial services; education, government and social services; engineering; health care; hospitality, entertainment and media; sales and personal services; and science.

Based on data from the U.S. Bureau of Labor Statistics' projections to 2006 and the bureau's *Occupational Outlook Handbook*, I list the best jobs, the ones with the highest percentage growth into the next decade.

- **Information technology:** Computer engineer, systems analyst, electronic data processor, software designer, computer technician, Web page manager, computer equipment repairer, database manager, research development specialist, drafter. Though many people have earned important and well-paying jobs in information technology without gaining college degrees, employers now are looking for applicants with advanced education, particularly with four-year college degrees in computer technology and information systems. Business, mathematics, and engineering degrees also are acceptable. Other requisites: The ability to think logically; to work in teams as well as being self-motivated; creativity; problem-solving skills; and strong oral and written communication skills.

- **Business and financial services:** Accountant, auditor, financial manager, administrative assistant (but not secretary), bookkeeping clerk, lawyer, financial planner, consultant, bank marketer, management consultant, medical records technician, court reporter, insurance claims adjuster, real estate agent, underwriter, and temporary service worker. An undergraduate or graduate college degree or training and certification in the field are required. You must have experience, continued training in your field, and exceptional ability with numbers. Computer literacy, a logical approach to solving problems, and good sales and communication skills are essential. Being a self-starter is a plus.

■ **Education, government, and social services:** Social worker, human services worker, teacher, professor, child care worker, corrections officer, police officer, psychologist, counselor, and speech pathologist. These are the caring professions, and the No. 1 requirement is concern for other human beings. Highly specialized training is needed for most of these jobs, ranging from associate librarian degrees to doctorates. Because of the demanding work, emotional stability is needed. Second languages are an asset. Computer literacy is required.

■ **Engineering:** Computer engineer, project manager, electrical engineer, civil engineer, consulting engineer, industrial engineer, and mechanical engineer. A minimum of a bachelor's degree in engineering is required. Master's and doctorates are needed for high-skilled jobs. State licensing is required for some work, such as consulting. Reasoning ability, innovation, team work, and strong communication skills also are needed. Computer skills are basic.

■ **Health care:** Home care aide, physical therapy assistant and aide, medical assistant, medical doctor, physical therapist, occupational therapist, respiratory therapist, dental hygienist, registered nurse, orderly, licensed practical nurse, and gerontologist. These, too, are caring professions, and hiring managers look for people with both skills and compassion. Training ranges from on the job to medical degrees. Certification and licensing also are required. Communication skills are essential. Flexibility in adapting to and handling emergencies are important. Computer literacy is a plus.

■ **Hospitality:** Waiter, waitress, food preparation worker, receptionist, hotel manager, cook, chef, and counter clerk. Constant contact with the public is characteristic of these jobs — a friendly demeanor and genuine interest in the customer are important. You also need the ability to take orders, work well under pressure, get along with others, and to be able to do several things at once. An undergraduate degree is needed in order to get a job beyond entry level. Experience is a plus, but most employers will train the right person. Computer literacy is also a plus.

■ **Entertainment and media:** Electronic media journalist, editor, television producer, film director, technical director, public relations consultant, photographer, and marketing and advertising personnel. A college degree usually is required. Employers seek prior experience in areas of the media — even with college publications. Knowledge of the English language, especially grammar and spelling, are basic. Creativity, being a self-starter, the ability to meet deadlines, good people skills, and confidence are needed. Computer literacy is a must.

■ **Sales and personal services:** Retail salesperson, cashier, cosmetologist, insurance agent, wholesale salesperson, sales manager, and telemarketer. Licensing and registration required for cosmetologist and insurance agent. An undergraduate degree is extremely helpful but not required for sales jobs. Good communication skills, good work ethic, being a self-starter, and an understanding of human behavior are important. A knowledge of the market you want to serve helps nail the job. Computer literacy is an asset.

■ **Sciences:** Chemist, physicist, food science technicians, environmental scientists, biologist, and criminologist. Four-year degrees to doctorates are required in these jobs. The ability to do research and think creatively also are sought by employers. Strong mathematical and analytical skills and computer knowledge are vital. Most of the jobs require working alone, setting your own schedule, and meeting your own goals.

Table 2-1 also lists the projected number of new jobs between 1996 and 2006, according to the Bureau of Labor Statistics Industry-Occupation Matrix. For more information, check out its Web site at `stats.bls.gov`.

Table 2-1   Projected Number of New Jobs Available between 1996 and 2006

Information Technology	New Jobs	Total Opportunities Today
Systems analyst	249,747	519,599
Computer engineer	170,542	235,299
Computer programmer	130,796	129,226
Database administrator, computer support, and other computer scientists	80,835	249,216
Data processing equipment repairer	34,233	Not available
Data entry keyers (noncomposing)	24,602	34,794
Drafter	1,094	7,023

Business and Financial Services	New Jobs	Total Opportunities Today
Financial manager	146,408	Not available
Lawyer	82,056	118,369
Paralegal	76,218	76,426
Accountants and auditors	49,176	124,551
Medical records technician	44,480	Not available
Insurance adjusters, examiners, and investigators	38,005	Not available
Real estate agent underwriter	15,537	Not available

Business and Financial Services	New Jobs	Total Opportunities Today
Court reporter/stenographer	4,574	Not available
Accounting, auditing, and bookkeeping clerks	4,546	Not available

Education, Government, and Social Services	New Jobs	Total Opportunities Today
Teacher (elementary, secondary)	449,070	Not available
Child-care worker	299,188	Not available
Teachers, special education	240,655	Not available
Social worker	187,563	Not available
College/university faculty	162,343	Not available
Human services worker	98,439	Not available
Police patrol officers	73,341	Not available
Vocational teachers/instructors	48,863	Not available
Teachers, preschool and kindergarten	25,709	Not available
Counselor	19,352	Not available
Speech pathologists and audiologists	18,102	Not available
Psychologist	11,381	Not available
Librarian	7,338	Not available
Police detectives and investigators	5,436	Not available

Engineering and Architectural Services	New Jobs	Total Opportunities Today
Civil engineer	22,189	
Electrical engineer	17,699	

(continued)

**Table 2-1   Projected Number of New Jobs
Available between 1996 and 2006
(continued)**

Engineering and Architectural Services	New Jobs	Total Opportunities Today
Mechanical engineer	10,913	
Computer engineer	9,155	
Industrial engineer	1,488	15,690

Health and Allied Services	New Jobs	Total Opportunities Today
Physical therapist	12,872	81,104
Registered nurse	12,430	410,394
Physical therapy assistant/aide	5,983	66,372
Licensed Practical nurse	4,540	148,394
Medical doctor (physician)	4,494	117,539
Occupational therapist	4,135	37,899
Medical assistant	3,389	166,352
Nursing aides, orderlies, and attendants	2,492	332,997
Respiratory therapist	506	37,464
Home care aide	Not available	171,396
Dental hygienist	Not available	64,015

Hospitality	New Jobs	Total Opportunities Today
Receptionist/info clerk	318,474	Not available
Cook	300,477	Not available
Food prep worker	233,917	Not available
Waiter/waitress	206,081	Not available
Hotel manager	1,420	Not available

Entertainment and Media	New Jobs	Total Opportunities Today
Editors and writers, including technical	60,713	Not available
Producers, directors, actors, and entertainers	24,828	Not available
Photographer	23,187	Not available

Sales and Personal Services	New Jobs	Total Opportunities Today
Cashier	530,065	Not available
Retail salesperson	408,253	Not available
Marketing and sales supervisors	246,341	Not available
Cosmetologist	57,937	Not available
Insurance agent	16,920	Not available
Wholesale buyer	9,114	Not available

Sciences	New Jobs	Total Opportunities Today
Biologist	20,690	Not available
Chemist	16,650	Not available
Foresters and conservation scientists	6,430	Not available
Agricultural and food scientists	4,764	Not available
Physicists and astronomers	-290	Not available

If a job appeals to you and you feel you aren't completely qualified right now to fill it, pursue it anyway: Many companies will train an attractive candidate, and you also can take qualifying courses on your own.

Moving away from fields that are not growing

Understanding which fields are expected to grow isn't enough. You also have to know which professions and industries are declining to avoid honing your skills and experience for a specific job — and then having to repeat the process in five years. For example, durable-goods manufacturing has been hit hard by a global economy where off-shore workers can produce the same products for less. This has resulted in production being shifted overseas and an influx of lower-cost imports. At the same time, the strong dollar versus other currencies has caused demand to weaken for U.S. exports.

Manufacturing employment continues to fall, particularly in the industrial machinery and equipment, electronic and electrical equipment and — continuing two decades of decline — textile mill products and apparel sectors. Mining employment also has decreased steadily in recent years. The construction, agriculture, forestry, and fishing industries are included in the goods-producing sector and are expected to need slightly more employees in the next decade.

There are good jobs in the construction, agriculture, forestry, and fishing industries, but these fields don't have the potential for dramatic growth that other sectors of the economy have.

The following jobs are expected to decline in the next decade:

- Material movers, clerical staff, and auditing clerks
- Excavation and loading machine operators, grader operators, and welders
- Industrial truck and tractor operators, blue-collar workers, supervisors, and electricians
- Crushing and mixing machine operators, general managers, and weighers and measurers

- Geologists, roustabouts, and inspectors

- Sewing machine operators, cannery workers, and dairy processing equipment operators

- Prepress workers, machine tool cutters, and reservation and transportation ticket agents

- Meter readers, directory assistance operators, and telephone repairers

- Stock clerks, tobacco workers in factories and agriculture, and jewelry designers

- Railroad workers, bank tellers, and computer operators

- Secretaries and bartenders

Warning

If you know you could be the best bartender in the world and, although the number of bartender jobs are declining, if you feel you can get a job as one, do it!

Gathering Information about a Job

As you get closer to a decision about what job will be the best for you, try to get some hands-on information about the nitty-gritty of what's involved and the typical work environment. Before you start out on your actual job search, try to find out in advance what it's like to do the job you think may be right for you. You can use several techniques to accomplish this.

Informational interviewing

Informational interviewing is one of the tools that will help you determine whether you're headed in the right direction. It involves talking to a professional already working in the field in which you're interested — preferably in person but over the phone is a good second best — and asking questions about job responsibilities, hours, salary, a typical day, and any other inside information you can glean.

An informational interview is not a job interview and should not be confused with one. You're seeking information, not a job — and you have to make that clear from the beginning, in order to put the interviewer at ease.

Don't be shy about calling any contact you might have, or even someone you don't know, to request a one-on-one conversation about the job you're interested in. Promise you will take only a few minutes of their time and won't ask for a job — and keep your promise. Hopefully, you'll be invited to come to the work site to have your discussion there. Even a brief visit will give you important information about your future work environment.

It's okay to ask the person you're talking to for names of people in the company who are responsible for hiring. But don't press too hard on this one.

Job shadowing

Job shadowing is a relatively new tactic to help job seekers examine possible positions up close and personal — and a very effective method of finding out in advance whether this is the right job for you. Job shadowing is just that: You follow someone currently doing the job you're interested in for any amount of time — from an hour to a full day — to find out what the job actually entails.

Job shadowing, which gives you access, information, and contacts, must be carefully planned in advance.

Viewed as a search method step that falls after informational interviews and before internships, it's usually up to you to arrange your brief visit by calling the company's human resource department or asking friends and other contacts to give you a few minutes in their day. Some college career placement centers will help students line up companies and professional contacts.

If you're unsuccessful in arranging a shadowing session, first ask for a brief informational interview during which you bring up the subject of shadowing.

Volunteering

Volunteer work is another way to get inside companies you might otherwise have no access to. Nonprofit organizations welcome such unpaid assistance, and, in addition to doing good, you'll have the opportunity to do the work that interests you. Nonprofits have almost every job for-profit businesses offer, so they provide a chance to observe the inner workings of the group while you're helping, to learn valuable skills, and possibly to meet people who may be willing to help with your future job hunt.

Pick a nonprofit agency involved in something you really care about, from college alumni departments to zoos. You'll be more enthusiastic and excited by your work if you believe in it.

Working on internships

Whether paid or unpaid, internships provide actual work experience to put on your resume, invaluable contacts, and unparalleled insights into determining the right job for you. They're temporary jobs — highly prized ones — for a few weeks to as long as a year in which you are taught the basics of the job and asked to help out wherever possible.

If you're enrolled in any type of educational program, ask your instructor or department head to arrange an internship for you in an area that interests you. If you're currently employed, you'll probably have to design your own internship, one that you can do evenings, weekends, or during vacations for a short period of time. Approach companies on your own about how you can help them and how they can help you.

Interviewing for an internship is serious business. Be prepared with your resume, interests, activities, and a list of what you can do to be of help and what you want to learn.

When you do your internship, be prepared to be the gofer, Jack or Jill of all trades, and the one everyone else feels free to boss around. Do whatever is asked of you and work hard. A strong reference from your internship provider will pay off later in your job search — and will be a vital part of your resume.

CHAPTER 3

DOING YOUR HOMEWORK

- Determining what you need to research for your job search

- Discovering where to go to answer all your job search questions

In this information age, facts are one of your most important tools for finding out what jobs are available in your field and which companies are looking for your skills and expertise. Without the necessary data on today's employment opportunities, you'll be operating in the dark and will prolong unnecessarily the duration of your job search. Your chances of finding the best job for you will be severely limited.

Being fully informed in advance of launching your job search will help you focus on where you want to work and ultimately will heighten your desirability to employers.

Doing Your Homework

Doing your homework is market research — and you're the product. You must do it to avoid making a disastrous mistake that will leave you frustrated, spinning your wheels, and even worse, jobless. The information you are able to glean by your own sweat equity will help make you aware of what's happening in the real world of work. You need to know exactly what's going on so that when you actually apply for a job you'll have already maximized your chances of getting it. Doing your homework helps you develop a smart marketing strategy for your job search.

Basic questions to ask

You'll want to find answers to some basic questions. Ask yourself the following questions to begin your research. If you're not sure how to find the answers, make sure that you read the next section, "Finding the Answers."

- Which industries have the most jobs in your field?

- Which companies in those industries are doing the most hiring?

- What is the present financial health of each of these companies?

- Are any of them contemplating expanding or downsizing in the near future?

- Are any of them ripe for takeovers?

- Who actually does the hiring in your field or department?

- What are the basic skills the hiring executives of these companies seek in someone in your field or function?

- What are the stated corporate values?

- Which companies offer the best salaries and best opportunities for advancement?

- Which companies provide the best opportunities for training and acquiring transferable skills?

- What are the geographical areas of the United States that have the most jobs in your field?

Compatibility questions to ask

In addition to the fundamental questions just listed, you'll also want to answer some basic personal questions. The following questions help you consider your compatibility with the companies you're researching. If you're not sure how to find the answers, make sure that you read the next section, "Finding the Answers."

- What companies have the best working environment for you?

- Which of the cities and states with the most jobs in your field are where you want to live?

- At which firms do you currently have the most personal and professional contacts?

- At which firms do you think you will best fit in?

- Where do you think you will have the best chances for success?

- At which companies do you think you will have the best chances of getting the benefits you want, equal opportunity promotions, and flexible working conditions, if you need them?

- At which firms do you think you are most likely to be happy?

- Are you willing to move? Is your family willing? If so, what type of area would you want to live in? What correlation is there between the job you want, the demand for it, and your desired destinations?

Warning

Don't be haphazard in your efforts to answer these vital questions. Keep careful notes, ask questions that are to the point, and find out as many answers as possible. Also, create a manageable schedule to do your research — and follow it.

Finding the Answers

Keep a folder or a computer file on each of the companies you're currently researching. Make a list of the top five businesses, government agencies, and nonprofit organizations that appeal to you as your first choices of the places you want to work. They are known as your *A List* — your top priority for heavy-duty research.

But just to hedge your bets, also make a list of the next five organizations you're interested in and start collecting information on them, too. They're your *B List* — your backup choices to study. These potential employers will be helpful not only in making decisions about where you ultimately want to apply for a job, but as you find out more about them, you may decide to move some of them into your A List.

Don't research more than ten companies at a time. Too much information can be stressful and overwhelming. In addition, focus on your A List.

Using the Internet

One of your best sources of information, but not the only one, is the Internet. By using keywords and the power of Internet search engines, you can quickly locate Web sites that can tell you more about potential jobs and specific employers. By the time you're done, you will probably have visited many career, job-search, corporate, government directory, and other sites as part of your research on the World Wide Web. You also might subscribe to newsgroups or visit chat rooms to talk with fellow job seekers or people in your field. You'll quickly pick up much of the information you need without making a phone call or leaving your chair. The data you acquire will help you to target the companies you want to know more about and answer your professional and personal questions.

At this time, you should be using the Internet to acquaint yourself with the culture of various companies, their financial condition, and the kind of jobs they're trying to fill. You're not ready to look for a specific job yet.

I always advise job seekers to begin their search on the Web by calling up America's Job Bank at www.ajb.dni.us. This Web site is a national treasure, maintained by the U.S. Department of Labor and coordinated by the 50 state employment services. America's Job Bank is updated daily and has an average listing of half a million jobs. It gives you excellent insight into the current employment demand of the U.S. labor market and where you fit in.

America's Job Bank shows you which jobs are the most plentiful and which states and cities have the most opportunities. It also will be an important source when you start your actual job search. (I go into greater detail on that in Chapter 4.) But right now, take advantage of its listings of job opportunities by specific professions and by geographical locations to pinpoint opportunities.

Just browsing through the various links of the government's Web site quickly gives you a snapshot of the following:

- What kinds of companies are most actively recruiting
- Where the best jobs are located nationwide
- The skills employers are looking for
- What kind of salaries are being offered
- Where your chosen profession fits into the current and future labor market.

America's Job Bank represents only a microcosm of U.S. employers and the data you need. But that microcosm is an essential part of your homework — particularly if you find out there aren't many job openings in your field or in the areas of the country in which you want to live.

Using the Internet is a fast way to access company reports and other "insider" information on how those organizations are doing. Up-to-date financial data is at your fingertips on the Internet at sites such as Bloomberg, Bridge, Hoover's, and *The Wall Street Journal.*

As you study these sites, start compiling a list of possible contacts from names you read on your screen, especially those of potential hiring managers in your area.

Include Web sites of colleges, universities, and nonprofit organizations in your search for information on your particular job and the industry it's in. And keep a record of the names, addresses, and phone numbers of professional associations in your field both nationally and locally so you can contact them as necessary.

If you don't have a personal computer at home or don't have access at your fingertips to the various data banks, put aside time to go to your college library or local public library. Helpful librarians are on hand to show you how to use their computers and how to get the information you need.

Using the library

Your nearest library, either a school, corporate reference, or public library, holds information you need to know about the job market. One of the best attributes of libraries, as compared to Web sites, is that human beings — caring professionals — usually are on hand to help you find the information you seek and to suggest places to look for data that you simply didn't know existed. Librarians can be personal guides for your job search.

Hands-on assistance from librarians will enable you to uncover whatever information you need about organizations where you might want to work and which might hire you.

Ask the librarian on duty for help in finding:

- Online databases that are pertinent to your job search
- Corporate annual reports
- Business publications, including newspapers and magazines
- Reference books
- Government reports
- Professional associations

Be courteous and considerate of the librarians you ask for help. You'll need them repeatedly when your actual job search begins.

Using the media

While you're conducting your job search, read at least one newspaper every day. By doing so, you'll be informed about what's going on in the world. Remember, the U.S. economy is part of a global marketplace that directly affects you. Actually, you should want to know what's going on in the world because the knowledge you acquire will help you make intelligent, informed decisions and make you a much more interesting job candidate.

Your local daily newspaper will keep you up-to-date on your area's business news. *The Wall Street Journal* will do the same on both a national and international level. Reading every book you can get your hands on about your profession and the companies in it will also give you a leg up over other job candidates.

Business magazines, which usually appear weekly, are another important source of information. And, for a sharper focus on your own field, review magazines, reports, and research published by professional associations for answers to many of your questions and additional insights from the people actually doing the job.

If you haven't done so already, now is the time to join professional associations and network in your field.

Watching television shows with daily business reports gives you an invaluable national and global picture of the economy and where your chosen profession fits in. Another source that's easy to tune into from your home are television news programs, which also are sources of important information that affect the economy and, therefore, the labor market.

Talk to everyone — friends, colleagues, acquaintances, neighbors, relatives, salespeople, supermarket cashiers, gas station attendants, even strangers on the bus. Find out what they know about the current job market or the companies you're researching. And remember, you owe them back at some future date.

CHAPTER 4
THE JOB SEARCH

IN THIS CHAPTER

- Beginning your well-researched job search

- Joining and participating in professional organizations for job tips and networking opportunities

- Using all the resources: Job clubs, job fairs, headhunters, and more

- Knowing what to do when you're employed and actively looking for a job

Now that you know what industry you want to work in and what companies have jobs you're interested in and qualified to perform, you're ready to begin your job search. It could take anywhere from three months to a year to find the right job, depending on your salary range, but the harder you work on your search, the shorter it will be. Keep in mind that the higher your salary, the longer it will take to find employment.

A job search is exhausting, physically and emotionally, particularly if you're already employed. It's a full-time job in itself, so make sure that you take good care of yourself during it: Exercise, eat well, get plenty of rest, and be good to yourself.

Beginning Your Search

Reading classified ads, telephoning potential employers, and using the Internet are important ways to find jobs.

Using classified ads

The classified ads are your best source for job opportunities, whether you're looking for a job in for-profit businesses, non-profits, or governmental agencies and whether you're seeking a part-time or full-time job. Most people get their jobs by answering a want ad. Follow these tips if you're using classified ads:

- Read your local paper every day.

- If you're looking for a job in another city, go to your public library and ask for that town's newspaper or look for it on the Internet.

- Follow up with phone calls, when possible, to seek specifics about the job. Don't hesitate to ask questions — and don't be afraid of rejection.

Classified ads have a short shelf life, so if any of them look interesting, follow up immediately with a phone call, where possible.

Though everyone talks about the importance of the Internet in a job search — and I do, too — there's nothing like direct contact such as a telephone call to jump-start your first personal connection with an identified potential employer.

Using the telephone

Here are ways to use the phone to get information about job openings, an interview, or permission to send a resume:

- Use your contacts and also call the company human resources department for information.

- Keep your call brief and focused. Don't waste anyone's time.

- Make sure that you're talking to the actual hiring officer, not the human resources department.

- Ask pertinent questions about the job and its responsibilities. This is not the time to discuss salary or benefits.

- Ask whether there's a specific kind of candidate they're looking for.

- Ask how to arrange an interview and to whom to send a resume.

- Thank them for their time.

Using the Internet

Though only a small percentage of job seekers actually get a job through the Internet — and most of the posted jobs, not surprisingly, are in information technology — the share is growing. Increasingly, employers are using the Internet to recruit workers of all types by posting jobs on commercial and/or government-operated career sites, and advertising for workers on their own Web sites. Because of the abundance of listings on the Internet, hunting for work via computer is a particularly good strategy for first-time job seekers and career changers who may have more job options than more experienced and specialized employees.

Tip

Though there is no guarantee you will get a job through the Internet, an advantage of using the Web is that it's fast and literally has millions of listings.

Start your job search by accessing major online job sites such as CareerPath at `www.careerpath.com` (see Figure 4-1), CareerMosaic at `www.careermosaic.com` (see Figure 4-2), Monster at `www.monster.com`, and America's Job Bank at `www.ajb.dni.us`. Like classified ads, openings posted on these job boards usually have a short shelf life, so you should promptly follow up on the jobs that interest you.

Figure 4-1: CareerPath.

Figure 4-2: Career Mosaic.

Tapping into company Web sites is another rich source of job opportunities. Because you already have a list of the companies you're interested in, you know which keywords to use to search their job banks. The advantage of company Web pages is that their job openings usually are current and give you exact information about how to apply for them. Follow their directions.

In order to get directly to the jobs you want to know about, be as specific as possible in your keyword searches and narrow as much as possible the parameters of your search.

Using your college's resources

If you're an undergraduate, a graduate, or someone just taking a few continuing education courses, your school is a treasure chest of job opportunities. Even if your college or university isn't near your home, telephone its career placement center to find out what jobs in your field or function are listed with it. Next, call the head of the department of the subject you majored in or currently are studying and ask for names and phone numbers of employers with job openings. Finally, if you can, visit the career center and the department head in person to make sure that you're getting every available listing and that the professionals involved know you're very serious about getting a job.

Many alumni who are successful in business go back to the schools they graduated from when they're looking for top talent. They know they got a good education and that current students and graduates whom their alma mater recommends also will be well qualified.

Joining Professional Organizations

If you don't already belong to at least one or two professional organizations in your field, join one. You can find them listed in the *Encyclopedia of Associations*. Professional organizations usually cost several hundred dollars to join, but they are worth every penny. They offer job banks, inside information, and career assistance.

Using job banks

Most associations have up-to-date job banks that list opportunities submitted by employers and members of the organization. It's a good place for employers to advertise if they're in the market for someone skilled and qualified because joining a professional organization shows intelligence, commitment, and a willingness on the part of a job seeker to seek and share knowledge.

Joining a professional group allows you to run your own advertisement seeking employment. Advertising to this targeted market — your association peers and their employers — is a powerful search tool both on a national and local basis. Additionally, many of the local chapters of national organizations send monthly mailings of job openings and jobs wanted.

Remember

Employers often simply pick up the phone and call professional associations to ask for recommendations for job openings. Make sure that your association knows you're in the job market, whether or not you place an ad in its publication.

Getting the word out at meetings

Professional associations offer you another important job tool: The opportunity to attend their meetings, conference, and seminars. Now is the time to attend them and talk with others about your quest. Showing up at these events is an investment that pays off because you'll get the inside track on job openings in your field. You may feel more relaxed about talking about your search goals if you remember that members of associations are committed to helping each other.

Warning

No one will know you're job hunting unless you tell them, so tell them. Remember that your fellow association members currently work in the fields with jobs you're looking for.

Stand up at meetings and announce out loud that you're looking for a job and ask these questions.

- Is your company planning to expand?
- Do you know of anyone who might leave his present job?
- Will you introduce me to the hiring officers at your firm?

Trying Other Methods

You can also find leads for your job search in several other ways, including job clubs, job fairs, headhunters, and employment agencies.

Job clubs

The whole is greater than the sum of its parts — and that's the theory underlying job clubs. A *job club* is a group of people — five is the minimum for effectiveness — who meet at least once a week to give each other support and confidence, exchange information about who is hiring, and to energize each other to continue on with a job search. Each job club member is responsible for the success and good spirits of other members.

Job clubs are sponsored by state employment services, churches, professional associations, libraries, community organizations, career-counseling services, groups of retired executives, YMCAs, and YWCAs. Because nonprofit groups usually run them, the job clubs are often free or only charge a nominal fee.

The groups have varied agendas, but most provide job hunting tips, career planning advice, and scheduled speakers, who include hiring officers, career counselors, and other experts. Qualified career and human resources personnel lead the meetings.

If you feel you would benefit from the direct support of a job club but can't find one that fits your needs, form your own from among your own friends and acquaintances who are job hunting. You'll be surprised how easy it is to find willing participants.

If you form your own job club it is up to you and the other members to do the organizational work, find a meeting place, set the rules, bring in helpful speakers, and keep each other motivated until every member has a job.

Job fairs

You may have attended job fairs when you were doing your homework in order to pick up inside information. But when you're involved in your actual job search, attending a job fair becomes a very serious matter. Employers participate in job fairs and pay for the right to be there because they need qualified employees. They mean business — and so should you.

Prepare for a job fair as you would if you were going to a job interview. Bring resumes, business cards, a notebook, and lots of confidence with you to the job fair. Dress professionally. Prepare the questions you want to ask. Be friendly and try to be relaxed. Get as many names as possible of contact people for future use.

Pick the job fairs you want to attend based on which employers will be there. You usually can find out this information by reading ads or by calling the job fair sponsors. Plan which companies you want most to visit at the job fair and create a timetable for stopping at their booths. If it's a large fair, you won't be able to get to everyone, so pick and choose among those that are your best bets. Try to talk to representatives of at least ten companies in a day.

Your purpose in attending a job fair is to line up a job interview with a company you're interested in.

Ask each representative for a listing of different positions the company has open, but even if you are interested in several of them, apply for only one at a time. Otherwise, you won't be taken seriously for any of them.

Follow up immediately on all job leads and contacts by calling the next day.

Headhunters

Executive recruiters — also known as *headhunters* — work for employers in corporations and nonprofit organizations to find the best candidates for their job openings.

Headhunters do not find you jobs. They do not work for you. They work for employers, who pay their bills. What they do is find qualified prospects, interview them, and present them to clients. If you use the following steps to get on a recruiter's radar screen and if you meet the job requirements, you may be contacted.

A few thousand executive recruiting firms handle tens of thousands of job openings a year, most of them at a salary level beginning at $75,000 annually. Many only recruit candidates for jobs paying upwards of $100,000. Corporations often turn over searches for their top jobs — from CEO on down — to executive recruiters, who do the ground work by finding qualified people for the job. Recruiters do no hiring; instead, they recommend a slate of up to five people for the job, after doing the necessary screening.

Headhunters, however, are invaluable because they're on top of the employment market — they have to be to earn their living. If a recruiter calls you, respond immediately and enthusiastically. You can learn a lot from recruiters because their knowledge about your field is both general and specific. They know who's hiring, what salary and benefits are being offered, and opportunities for advancement at individual companies. They also know the exact requirements of the job they're trying to fill and why the position is open.

You don't have to wait for a recruiter to contact you. Find out the names of those in your field by doing a keyword search on the Internet or contacting your professional association and asking for a list of headhunters. When you contact an executive recruiter, ask for a meeting. Send them your resume to keep on file (see Chapter 6 for more on writing a resume). Keep in frequent contact with one or two executive recruiters during your job search.

Use headhunters wisely — as they will use you. If you don't get a job interview at least get as much inside information as you can. Have your questions ready when you meet or talk by phone.

While it's important to have a good relationship and to cooperate completely with headhunters during your job search, don't depend on them to place you in a job. Even if your candidacy is proceeding well and the recruiter is optimistic you are the person for the job, you don't want to put all your eggs in one basket. Keep looking elsewhere.

Employment agencies, temporary services, and part-time work

Employment agencies find people jobs, and if you fear your job search isn't going anywhere, you might want to respond to one of their advertisements. But they, too, work for the client — not for you. Because rapid turnover in filling jobs is the way they make money — most are not paid by clients unless the job is filled — your skills and interests are not as important as they are to an executive recruiter. If you need a job in a hurry and an employment agency has some in your field, it's an avenue to consider.

Never accept a job with an employment agency that requires you to pay any or all of the fee. You don't want to work for an employer that expects the job seeker to pay for the job.

Temporary agencies are an excellent way to get back into the job market if you've been out of it for a while. They provide training and access to permanent employment for clerical, manufacturing, and professional employees. A drawback is that most temp agencies pay low hourly wages and require temps on their payrolls to work an extended period before they qualify for such benefits as healthcare and vacation time. Many people take temp jobs during their job search to keep money coming in and to add an additional reference to their resume.

If you like your temporary job and if the employer likes you, your temporary agency, after a few months, might be able to negotiate your transfer to a full-time employee of the client company.

Like temporary work, a part-time job is a comfortable segue to a full-time job with a future. It gets you in the door of a targeted employer, and from there you can position yourself to get the full-time job you want.

The U.S. Bureau of Labor Statistics reports that "much of the hiring done by fast-growing industries . . . is for part-time positions."

Networking

Getting on the telephone or talking in person to your personal and professional contacts is an important way to find a job that's right for you. Make a list of people you know in the field in which your looking for a job as well as the companies you're interested in and tell them directly: "I'm job hunting. What do you know?" Ask them to keep their eyes and ears open for you and to tell their friends and colleagues you're looking for a job.

CHAPTER 5

CREATING YOUR TICKET TO SUCCESS: THE RESUME

IN THIS CHAPTER

- Knowing what to include in your resume
- Understanding the three main types of resumes
- Creating and tightening up your best resume

Before you can answer an employment ad that appeals to you or ask a potential employer for a job interview, you must have an up-to-date resume detailing the jobs you've held, the experience you've gained, and your education and training.

At this point in your job search, you need a current and focused account of your professional history, a *baseline resume* — one that you can adapt to various jobs and various employers as your search progresses.

Your resume is another important tool for you to see exactly what you've done and the skills you've acquired.

It doesn't sound too complicated, but many job seekers panic at the thought of compiling a resume. Yet, the process of putting together a written presentation that shows why you are the best candidate for the job is simply a matter of logic. Your resume, which is your entry to the job interview you so avidly desire, can be created quickly and simply, without sweat or tears.

Your resume is not your life history on paper. Instead, it's a focused marketing tool, a brief listing — on one page — of your relevant background and qualifications. Brief resumes are a plus because personnel managers and recruiters are pressed for time.

Remember that your resume gets the ball rolling by helping you to get the job interview. Though it gives you an enormous assist, it doesn't get you the job itself.

Put your ego aside when preparing your resume. Include only what potential employers really want, even if you've done a million other wonderful things.

To Reveal or Not to Reveal

You should never include some things in a resume, some because they work against you, others because they're not relevant, and still more you shouldn't reveal because it may cause employers to discriminate against you when hiring. While laws protect candidates from discrimination, you want to avoid having to take employers to court.

In creating a resume, you only want to include data that will help you get the job interview and not rule you out. Too much information will only confuse hiring officers — if they read all of it, that is.

Personal items you don't want to mention

Never mention your gender, race, age, religion, ethnic background, or your health status or that of your dependents. Because you cannot guess in advance the possible prejudices or preferences of a potential employer, do not include a photo. These issues have nothing to do with your qualifications for a job. Don't reveal whether you're married, have a family, plan to have a family, are pregnant, are willing to travel, are divorced, or are a single parent. These matters can be discussed legally after the job offer is made.

Don't include jobs you've held for less than a year that have no bearing on the position you're seeking. Mention them in the job interview to explain the time gaps — if you're asked about them.

What about volunteer work?

Omit details about volunteer activity, unless the experience you gained from it pertains to the job you're applying for. Don't include information about community or political activity; college activities; sports you play; and important friends or other connections you might have. This is the kind of information — except for political activities, which never should be mentioned — you can bring up and use to market yourself in the job interview.

What about why I'm job hunting?

Never include anything about why you're looking for a new job, why you left your last one, or why you want to leave your present one. These questions also will come up in the job interview, and I'll help you answer them in Chapter 8. Also, leave out any mention of references — that information also comes later.

What about salaries?

Many ads for jobs ask you to include your salary history and requirements with your resume — but at the same time, the ads do not indicate the salary range the employer is considering. That puts you in an unfair bargaining position from the get-go and is the reason I strongly urge job applicants not to mention salary at all.

Listing your current salary or your salary expectations can rule you out of consideration for the job before you even get a shot at the interview because they may be too low or too high for the particular job.

Some potential employers are adamant about knowing how much money you now make and what you expect to make in the new job. Even in these cases, in order to avoid having your resume discarded before you get a chance to be interviewed in person, your best approach is to give a salary range, a very wide one, such as "in the $30,000's annually." In that way, you won't hurt your chances to get the salary you deserve when it comes to actual negotiations for pay and benefits (more about these negotiations in Chapter 9).

Before listing your salary range, research what the job actually pays by checking with those already in the field and with professional organizations.

Understanding the Three Types of Resumes

Employers tell me they hate to read resumes almost as much as job seekers hate to create them. But hiring professionals really aren't that difficult to please. They basically want the information they need without any frills — just the facts. They want everything on one page, where they can see what they need to know in one glance.

The three types of resumes that generally are acceptable by hiring officers are the *chronological,* the *skills* (or *functional*), and the *historical* (or *anecdotal*). I show you what these typical resumes look like so that you understand exactly what's expected, but no matter what work you've done or how diverse your background, your resume — whether on paper or via e-mail or the Internet — must have these ingredients:

- Your name, address, phone number, and e-mail address

- The job you're applying for or professional goal

- Your work experience

- Your educational background, including any scholastic honors, and pertinent awards

- What you can do for this company better than anyone else

When listing your work experience, be sure to indicate whatever new skills you learned at the various positions you held and your major accomplishments in each job. When listing your educational background, briefly note what you learned or excelled in that applies to the requirements of the job you seek.

The chronological resume (the one employers want most)

The most popular resume among employers is one that's a quick read of your background. The chronological resume (see Figure 5-1) includes your work experience in reverse chronological order (starting with your present job and going backward in time). It shows your experience, the key contributions you made to each employer, and the skills you acquired in each position. Employers like this format because it's easy to read, and they can quickly follow your work experience and detect any gaps.

It is the resume I recommend most strongly.

The skills or functional resume

The skills or functional resume is an important option for those who don't have the exact experience or educational background necessary for the job they want. The skills and experience listed emphasize your professional strengths in general that you believe to be transferable skills for the job you're applying for.

This type of resume is not as effective as a chronological resume because potential employers have to work harder to learn your relevant background.

The skills or functional resume has to show exactly what you can do for a particular employer, or it will be eliminated as a candidate.

Say, for example, that the job seeker, Jane Doe, wants that same marketing job applied for with the chronological resume, but in this case suppose that she has held few positions in the field and does not have a degree in marketing. Yet, she does have strengths and other educational experience that she believes will enable her to switch careers and do the job well. Under these circumstances, a skills or functional resume will serve her best.

Figure 5-1:   A sample baseline chronological resume.

Jane Doe
300 E. Elm St.
Chicago, IL 60611
312-777-8001
janedoe@aol.com

Objective: Marketing Director for XYZ Food Brands, Inc.

Experience

Marketing Director, Highland Advertising, Inc., Chicago, with annual sales of $1 billion. Responsible for 52 food products. Increased clients by 50 percent. Moved up from assistant marketing director in one year. Introduced promotional tie-ins. 1996 to Present.

Assistant Marketing Director, Good Stuff Foods Co., Cleveland, Ohio, with annual sales of $500,000. Responsible for supermarket displays. Increased exposure by 25 percent. Active in national retail organizations. 1989 to 1996.

Wholesale food representative, Diet Supplement Products, Inc., Chicago, with annual sales of $250,000. Responsible for selling vitamins to food stores and pharmacies. Increased sales by 10 percent annually. Wrote effective marketing pamphlets. 1982 to 1989.

Retail clerk, Mary's Boutique, Chicago. Sold women's clothing while going to college. Learned customer relations.

Education

University of Chicago, MBA, with specialty in marketing.

DePaul University, Chicago, Bachelor of Science in business. Graduated cum laude. President of college marketing club.

What I Can Do For You: I know food marketing from manufacturing to sales, have important professional and industry contacts, and can hit the ground running.

Remember

Keep the skills or functional resume (see Figure 5-2) as brief as possible to make sure that it will be read and also that the reader will not think you're trying to cover up your deficiencies.

The historical or anecdotal resume

To me, this form of resume is the resume of last resort: You want the potential employers to know — but there's a lot more you don't want them ever to know that a standard resume would reveal. The historical or anecdotal resume is a good fallback for people who have

■ Changed jobs often

■ Been fired or laid off often

■ Had a series of short-term jobs rather than long-term employment

■ Been out of the labor market for long periods of time

This type of resume (see Figure 5-3) works well for people who are good communicators, who can sell themselves in writing, who truly are enthusiastic about working for a particular company, and whose skills — if not job history — are beyond reproach. It differs from a cover letter, which briefly states why you are applying for a job, because it informally details your experience and education in a narrative way.

This resume, too, must be brief and to the point.

Figure 5-2:   A sample baseline functional (or skills) resume.

Jane Doe
300 E. Elm St.
Chicago, IL 60611
312-777-8001
janedoe@aol.com

Objective: Marketing Director for XYZ Brands, Inc.

Experience and Accomplishments

Creative work: Designed in-house publication for large manufacturing company resulting in increased worker loyalty. Planned effective sales campaign for national retail organization resulting in 25 percent increase in sales. Devised brochures and other sales literature for wholesale food market, increasing sales by 10 percent annually. Tracked success of point of sales techniques for sales manager.

Teamwork: Successfully worked on and led team projects in manufacturing and wholesale and retail sales. Motivated other team members to meet deadlines.

Supervisory: Headed a department of 10 people with increased productivity and no turnover in seven years. Met all goals and budgets every year.

Client contact: Successfully solicited and retained at least five new clients each year for wholesale food suppliers. Became well known nationally at retail stores by frequent client contact and through conferences and professional associations.

Employment

1996 to Present: Account Supervisor, Highland Advertising, Inc., Chicago.

1989 to 1996: Assistant Vice President of Sales, Good Stuff Foods Co., Cleveland.

1982 to 1989: Manager, team projects, Diet Supplement Products, Inc., Chicago.

1980 to 1982: Retail Clerk, Mary's Boutique. Sold women's clothing.

Education: Bachelor of Arts degree in psychology, DePaul University, Chicago. Editor of college paper. Graduated with honors. Speak fluent Spanish.

What Can I Do For You: With my strong communications skills, customer service abilities, sales experience, and professional contacts, I can hit the ground running.

This type of resume can't be filled with flowery statements and meaningless verbiage. It too, ultimately must give the necessary information to make potential employers want to interview you in person.

Say, for example, the same Jane Doe wants a marketing job at the same company. She's been out of the paid labor market for ten years raising her children, but now wants to go back to work in the same field she left a decade ago. Or, she was fired from her last job, downsized from the previous one, and stayed in two other jobs only six months each. As a result, she can't afford to be specific about the dates of her work experience.

But there are pluses: Doe has taken additional courses at night school and on weekends. She's done advertising, marketing, and public relations for her children's school and for a nonprofit social service agency in her community. She's not applying for the director's job. She knows that's beyond her at this point. She wants a job as marketing assistant. Her greatest strength: She is confident that she has a flair for the profession and can do a great job.

Figure 5-3: A sample baseline historical (or anecdotal) resume.

Jane Doe
300 E. Elm St.
Chicago, IL 60611
312-777-8001
janedoe@aol.com

To: James Jones
Marketing Director
XYZ Brands
311 Main St.
Chicago, IL 60614

Dear Mr. Jones,

I am a marketing professional with ten years experience at a Fortune 1000 food manufacturer and am responding to your ad for a marketing assistant for XYZ Brands. I have closely followed your fast-growing company and am uniquely qualified to respond to the challenges of such growth: In my last job, the budgets of marketing programs I worked on grew to $10 million from $1 million.

As a professional, I have proven that I can think strategically, handle special projects, meet deadlines, satisfy customers, and supervise and motivate team members. I have been successful in targeting, attracting, and keeping new clients both on a local and national basis. I have handled major accounts, conducted necessary research about their markets, and consistently improved their image and sales. I have done the same for community organizations on a volunteer basis.

One of my strongest accomplishments is successfully handling the launch of major new products, from helping create the concept of the product itself to fully developing the concept of how it will be marketed. One of my strongest attributes is my creativity.

I have a Bachelor of Science degree in economics and have taken college-level courses in computer technology, marketing, and communications. I work well with people and am a team player.

What I Can Do For Your Company: I know food marketing from product development to sales and can hit the ground running.

Sincerely yours,

Jane Doe

Even though the historical or anecdotal resume seemingly is informal, a cover letter still must accompany it.

Though these are the three basic forms of resumes that help get you in the door, they're not set in stone: You can improvise on each of them or use combinations of all three to help market yourself effectively.

CHAPTER 6
PACKAGING YOURSELF: THE COVER LETTER AND RESUME PRESENTATION

IN THIS CHAPTER

- Learning the dos and don'ts of cover letter content
- Creating the perfect cover letter for your resume
- Determining the best way to submit your cover letter and resume

If you know how to package and prepare a cover letter, your resume will be more likely to be read — and your chance of getting the job you want will be increased.

What a Cover Letter Can Do for You

A cover letter, combined with your resume, is your first written contact with a potential employer. It's the first thing that's read — even before the resume — and therefore is usually your first impression.

Your cover letter, like your resume, must be grammatically correct and without typos.

Here's why you need a good one and what it should include.

- To get the hiring officer interested enough in you to read your attached resume and set up a job interview

- To present credentials not included in your resume

- To give a glimpse into your personality

- To mention the name of an important contact, if you have one

- To request a personal interview

- To state you will follow up with a phone call

- To emphasize the confidentiality of your job application if you are presently employed

A cover letter is so important you should never submit a resume without one.

What a good cover letter does for you

Though it is the resume that employers concentrate on, the power of a cover letter is that it can be instrumental in their decision about whether they want to go on and read the resume at all. An impressive cover letter will distinguish you from other job applicants who submit run-of-the-mill cover letters. It will help keep your resume alive — and out of the waste basket. A good cover letter:

- Positions you as a serious job seeker

- Demonstrates that you have done your homework on the company and that you know its goals and values — and names and titles of those doing the hiring

- Underscores the information in your resume that shows how well your skills and attributes meet the needs of the job being offered and what you can do for the company

- Indicates your specific achievements in previous jobs

- Showcases your communication skills

■ Establishes you as a prospect who will be a self-starter from Day One

The cover letter must be individually tailored to each person or company you send your resume to. Each cover letter, unless you're answering a blind ad, must be addressed to the hiring officer — by name and title.

What to leave out of the cover letter

You should never include the following information in your cover letter.

■ Information about your experience, education, or other credentials that do not apply to the position that you want

■ What you hope the company can do for you

■ Any mention of references

■ How your family has always bought the company's products

■ That you're willing to take any job available

■ Anything that sounds like bragging

■ Information about your age, race, gender, religious or ethnic background, and marital status

■ Why you want to leave your present job or why you left the last one

Creating the Cover Letter

When writing your cover letter, keep your audience in mind. Your cover letter and resume are sent to potential employers in response to a specific request to see your resume; in answer to a published ad, either with the name of the potential employer or not; to executive recruiters; and to job banks.

Start by composing a cover letter that has the basic information in it that will best market you, and then tailor it to each specific person or place you send it to.

Despite the important information a cover letter has to include, it must be brief: Personnel executives don't have the time to read a lengthy introduction or general sales pitch. Keep it to a maximum of four short paragraphs, which will show you respect the reader's time. Don't be pretentious or use flowery language. Be yourself.

Tip

If you submit your cover letter by mail or fax, prepare it on a plain piece of white stationery, preferably your own business letterhead — not that of your current employer.

Cover letter for the chronological resume

Jane Doe, our job seeker in Chapter 5, created a baseline chronological resume. Figure 6-1 shows a baseline sample cover letter to accompany her resume.

Cover letter for the skills (or functional) resume

If you don't have the degrees or all of the skills the employer is looking for, you want to emphasize the business skills you do have that apply to the job opening. Figure 6-2 shows you a sample cover letter.

Cover letter for the historical (or anecdotal) resume

If you've been out of the labor market, unemployed for a while, or have changed jobs often — or frequently have been fired — your resume has an informal tone to avoid discussing the gaps in your employment. Your cover letter, therefore, also will have to be somewhat informal. Figure 6-3 shows you a sample one.

Figure 6-1:   Sample baseline cover letter for a chronological resume.

Jane Doe
300 E. Elm St.
Chicago, IL 60611
312-777-8001
janedoe@aol.com

(Today's Date)

John Smith
Executive Vice President, Marketing
XYZ Food Brands, Inc.
6000 W. Wacker Drive
Chicago, IL 60004

Dear Mr. Smith,

Mary Jane Johnson, your colleague at XYZ Food Brands, suggested I write to you about the opening you have for marketing director. I'm enclosing my resume for your consideration. I have almost 20 years experience in marketing and currently am marketing director for a $1 billion company with national distribution. Although the brands I currently represent do not compete with yours, much of our client base is similar. Last year, sales of the products I marketed increased by 25 percent.

I know from recent newspaper articles and other research that XYZ Food is planning a major expansion. I hope to be a productive part of this effort. As you will see from my resume, I have unique qualifications to do this job from the moment I'm hired.

As I am currently employed, I would appreciate your keeping this application confidential. I will call you in a few days to arrange a personal interview. Or, you can reach me at the above phone number or home or e-mail address. Thank you so much for your time.

Sincerely,

Jane Doe

Figure 6-2:   Sample baseline cover letter for a skills or functional resume.

Jane Doe
300 E. Elm St.
Chicago, IL 60611
312-777-8001
janedoe@aol.com

(Today's Date)

John Smith
Executive Vice President, Marketing
XYZ Food Brands, Inc.
6000 W. Wacker Drive
Chicago, IL 60004

Dear Mr. Smith,

I saw your ad for marketing director in today's *Chicago Tribune*, and this letter and enclosed resume are my application for that position. I have worked in advertising since 1982 and am known for my management skills, creative ideas, ability to motivate others, thorough follow-through, and my on-target marketing ideas. My current employer does some $10 million annually in sales. Each year, I have increased the earnings of each of my accounts.

I heard you speak on your company's plans for expansion last year at a seminar on marketing you gave at the local Chamber of Commerce. I even came up afterwards to congratulate you on your speech. Ever since, I have been following your company's progress and know I can be a productive part of it.

As I am currently employed, I would appreciate your keeping this application confidential. I will call you in a few days to arrange a personal interview. Or, you can reach me at the above phone number or home or e-mail address. Thank you so much for your time.

Sincerely,

Jane Doe

Figure 6-3:   Sample baseline cover letter for a historical or anecdotal resume.

Jane Doe
300 E. Elm St.
Chicago, IL 60611
312-777-8001
janedoe@aol.com

(Today's Date)

John Smith
Executive Vice President, Marketing
XYZ Food Brands, Inc.
6000 W. Wacker Drive
Chicago, IL 60004

Dear Mr. Smith,

I saw that you have an opening for a marketing assistant on your Web site and am applying for the job. Perhaps you remember me: We met in Denver last year at the annual convention of the National Association of Marketing Executives. We exchanged cards.

I have a decade of experience marketing food products and am respected in the industry. I have another important attribute: I also really know how to use computer technology and am the person everyone turns to at work when their computers fail.

I will be in touch with you in a few days to set up a personal interview. Or, you can reach me at the above phone number or home or e-mail address. Thanks so much for your time.

Sincerely,

Jane Doe

Modifying Your Cover Letter

Here are some helpful tips for special situations:

- If you're sending your resume to an executive recruiter, your cover letter should be brief but include this statement: "I am looking forward to working with you."

- If it's going to a job bank, to be included among its Jobs Wanted, state what category you want to be listed under.

- If you're responding to an ad, clearly indicate which ad you're referring to.

- If the job you're applying for or the hiring officer is in another city, state that you will be happy to go there for an interview at your own expense. If you will be in that town shortly, give the date and say that you will call in advance to see whether an appointment is possible.

- If you've called about an ad and were asked to submit a resume, state in your cover letter that "the enclosed information is in response to my telephone conversation today with you. Here's the resume you requested."

- If you're answering a blind ad, address it to Dear Sir or Madam, Dear Hiring Officer, or To Whom It May Concern.

Submitting Your Cover Letter and Resume

Sending your cover letter and resume, whether it's by mail, fax, or e-mail or posting it on a job bank on the Internet, is a formal business procedure. Put the date both on the cover letter and resume. Also, make sure that you tailor each resume to include the keywords that describe the skills, experience, and job the company is seeking. Today, most resumes — those not thrown away — are scanned into the company's computer database, and you want yours to be the one that's called up.

Resist any temptation to send your package by carrier pigeon, to step out of a cake with your resume in hand, or to put it in a helium balloon and have a clown deliver it. You may get attention but you won't get the job interview. Instead, keep everything businesslike.

After you tailor your resume and cover letter to the individual, company, or other source you're sending it to, you can send it by mail, fax, or e-mail , deliver it to the company personally, or post it on the Internet.

Delivering your cover letter and resume in person

It may sound old-fashioned in this high-tech age to physically hand in your cover letter and resume to the proper person, but, if you're in the geographical area, it is an extremely effective way of getting it there on time, safe and sound. Many personnel officers are impressed by a job applicant who actually shows up in person to submit a resume.

When you leave your documents, look around and see whether you can absorb any of the corporate culture. Also, try to make friends with the receptionist, secretary, assistant, or hiring officer who accepts it. This person can be an important contact and can come in handy later.

Mailing your cover letter and resume

Use a business envelope, but not your current employer's stationery. Accurately address it to the person or department it should go to. Telephone in a few days to see whether it was received. Most applicants use regular mail, but others, who want proof that the letter reached its destination, use a courier service, overnight, or certified mail. Some personnel officers pay more attention to the latter forms of mail delivery.

Faxing your cover letter and resume

Many classified ads, as well as interested employers, ask you to fax your resume. That means it will print out on a piece of white paper (perhaps even thermal paper — the shiny paper that comes on a roll), probably look like everyone else's, and will have to stand on its own merits. It will then most likely be scanned into the company's employment computer database.

Don't try to format your resume with flourishes, graphics, or fancy printing because the fax and/or computer may not be able to replicate them and your resume won't be readable.

After you fax your resume and cover letter, follow up with a phone call to make sure that it was received.

E-mailing your cover letter and resume

Often, hiring officers will ask you to e-mail your resume, a fast way to get it to the company. Send both your cover letter and resume *in the body of the e-mail itself.* Include your material in the text of the e-mail: Don't make your resume an attachment. Some companies, fearful of computer viruses, don't open attachments. Others may have software programs that aren't compatible with yours and won't be able to receive it. Once again, your electronic resume should be without whistles, bells, fancy lettering, bullets, graphics, or underlines — in other words, no elaborate formatting whatsoever.

Create a text document on a generic ASCII file to make sure that the receiving computer can receive it regardless of the word processing software it has been prepared with.

While some companies print out your cover letter and resume when they receive it via e-mail, more often electronic resumes are sent directly to the firm's database for storing.

The advantage of e-mailing your cover letter and resume is that it usually is sent directly to the company's database. You thereby avoid any problems that may arise from the recipient's being unable to scan it.

Though many companies have computer programs that send you an automatic acknowledgment of the receipt of your resume, still follow up with a phone call by sending a hard copy of your resume through the mail.

Posting your resume on the Internet

Sending your resume to career and corporate Web sites is an important step in your job search. Employers, who pay to be part of a job site or who bear the expense of maintaining a Web site, check them frequently for potential candidates.

When your resume appears on the Internet, you literally are telling the world you're looking for employment. If for any reason you want to keep your job search private, don't use the Internet. Also, your resume may be duplicated at other sites without your permission and may never actually be deleted from cyberspace.

Tailor your resume to each potential employer, job site, corporate Web site, nonprofit group, college, and university. As with an e-mail, keep it simple. Follow directions and make sure that it's in a format that is compatible with the site you're sending it to. Put a date on it before you post it and update it from time to time. Also, send a hard copy of your cover letter and resume — just in case.

Don't count on the Internet as your sole source of getting a job. The Internet is a powerful communication tool, but only a small percentage of job seekers get jobs from it, most of them information technology professionals.

Following Up

To make sure that your resume was received and to make an appointment for a job interview, telephone the potential employer a few days after your resume was transmitted. Keep calling once a week for at least three weeks, after that time only call if the ad for the job continues to appear. If you responded to a blind ad, send a follow-up letter within a few days indicating that you hope your resume was received and that you're available for an in-person job interview. If you don't have a private line at home, set up a dedicated phone line and answering machine to receive these calls.

The goal of your efforts is to get an interview, which, hopefully, will lead to a job. Press that point, without being overbearing, by suggesting days and times that you are available to meet.

CHAPTER 7

GATHERING REFERENCES: YOUR JOB INSURANCE

IN THIS CHAPTER

- Choosing the best references
- Handling a bad reference

Supplying a reference is a positive step forward in your job search because it means that there is a potential employer out there who is interested in you. If you and another job candidate have equally impressive resumes, references could be the factor that gives one of you the advantage.

But just as references can help you get the job you want, they can also completely sabotage your chances. That's why you can't leave the details of your obtaining references up to chance.

Compiling Your References

Compile a list of people you'd like to use as references. Contact eight to ten potential references so that you can mix and match them for individual employers.

Here's what to do:

- Actively recruit the people you want to serve as your references. (See the section "Gathering references," later in this chapter.)

- Ask their permission to put their names on your list.

- Ask them what they plan to say.

- Suggest to them what you want them to say, stressing that their role is to vouch for you as a professional.

Don't supply any references until you've been asked to come in for a job interview or know that you are a top candidate for the job, especially if you're currently employed. And when asked for your list, notify everyone on it that you've submitted their names and that they'll probably be hearing soon from the employer.

Compiling a list of references to tailor to each specific company and job is an ongoing process during your job search. Create your list, if possible, on your home computer. Put your name, address, and phone number at the top of it. Include each person's business title, address, and phone number, making sure that every name is spelled correctly, titles are up to date, and addresses and phone numbers are accurate. When employers request your references, select the names you want to use for that individual employer, print the list, and hand it in.

Securing the best references

Your selection of references must be based solely on those people who know your recent work accomplishments, your potential, and your character. They should be former employers, managers, or impressive individuals in your field or your community — people who actually know you.

Your strongest references are your current supervisor and employers you've worked for in the past five years — but only if they will give a positive recommendation.

Other important sources for references include

- A high-ranking executive in your company.

- Colleagues, particularly those who worked on teams or projects with you.

- Subordinates, if you've managed people.

- Supervisors of volunteer organizations for which you've worked on projects where you used or learned skills pertaining to the job you're seeking.

- Volunteers with professional credentials with whom you've volunteered.

- Members of the board — usually high-ranking executives — of volunteer organizations to which you belong.

- Professors, heads of departments, or workshop leaders who know your work.

These are good sources if you're just out of college and have little paid work experience.

- Directors of internship programs you've recently served in.

- People who like and respect you — but who are not related to you.

Gathering references

Before you give an employer your list, call each of your references, tell them you're giving their name as a reference, and ask whether they will be available over the next few months. Tell them how important their recommendation is to you personally. If you sense that a potential reference is offended by your asking exactly what they plan to say, eliminate that name from your list: You need your references to be fully supportive of you and to corroborate what you say about yourself in your resume and cover letter.

Asking someone to be your reference is a selling job. Be thorough in explaining the details of the position you're seeking, why you know it's a good fit for you, and how you're depending on this person's recommendation to get the job.

Hopefully, you'll get an enthusiastic or at least understanding response from the references you've selected. Most will ask either to meet with you or for a copy of your resume. Be professional, grateful, tactful — and agree to their requests.

Next, ask them what they will say in response to such questions about who they are, what they do, how long they've known you, what they know about you, and why they are recommending you. This also gives you an opportunity to reassess if they are the right references for the particular job you seek. Then, suggest what you would like them to say and why, but add that you will put it all in writing and will send a sample resume to them to use as background for their reply.

If a potential employer is concerned that you may not be qualified because of your lack of training in a specific skill, include among your references someone who can attest to your competency in that area and who will emphasize that you can do the work required.

Most references will ask you what you want them to say. Use that request as an opening to assure them that you know they'll do a wonderful job, but emphasize it would be very helpful to you if they would say certain things verbally or in a letter. Then, make your suggestions, but also follow up with a sample resume.

Don't be passive about securing references. You will have little control over your references and what they say unless you hand-pick them and describe the type of things you would like said about you.

Your references, who probably are busy people, will need time to organize and write a letter or to decide how they will respond to a telephone call about you. Give them as much advance notice as you can — you want them to be ready when the hiring officer calls.

When you talk to previous or current supervisors, it's essential to ask specifically what they plan to say about you. Because of concerns about lawsuits filed by former employees charging defamation of character, some employers only will give the dates you worked for them and nothing else — even if you were a highly valued employee. That's fairly standard but hardly a recommendation.

If you're currently employed and already have given notice, it's usually difficult to ask your manager, even a sympathetic and understanding one, to say certain things about you in a reference. Still, you must ask for the reference, and if your manager agrees, discuss what he or she plans to say, because you can't afford to leave this endorsement up to fate. If not, you'll have no idea what will be said, particularly if it's a phone reference.

Warning

Ask for a written letter of reference to take with you when you leave, addressed to "To Whom It May Concern." Because you will be able to read the reference, your manager may decide to be a little more generous in describing and recommending you. And the written letter may be so sufficient that your potential employer may not phone your manager after all — always an advantage when you quit a job.

If you find out your manager will not provide a potential employer with any information about your background or accomplishments, ask colleagues, team members, managers of other departments who know your work, and former executives of the company to be your reference. But keep your manager on the list because doing so implies you didn't leave your job in bad standing.

Don't lie to a potential employer and don't ask your references to lie for you, either. Ethics aside, you'll be caught.

Fighting a bad reference

One of the hardest things to ascertain is whether you're getting a bad reference. After you've been turned down for several jobs you feel you were qualified for and know that the job interview went well, a bad reference may be a strong possibility. Still, it is very hard to find out what your previous employer said or wrote and the hiring officer usually does not give out this information either.

Employers have protection from civil suits on defamation of character when their references are truthful. But there are a growing number of cases of former employees suing companies because their former bosses told lies about their honesty and character. Some of these employees are winning their suits by proving intentional falsehood and reckless disregard for the truth. But being involved in a lawsuit usually stalemates your job search for at least a year.

If you think you know who might be giving you a bad and false reference, ask a friend to call and request one. You might also want to talk to an employment lawyer about your options.

Keeping in Touch with Your References

A job search can take a long time, and you want to make sure that you are up to date on your references and that they are up to date on you. Keep in touch. Follow up with phone calls. Take them to lunch. Let them know how the search is going. Ask for advice. They'll be impressed with your earnestness and dedication in searching for a job, and it will reflect in their recommendations — no matter how long your search lasts.

Though it may be harder to do, keep in touch with your previous manager and colleagues if you've listed them as references.

Knowing you have the solid backup of people who will corroborate what you say about yourself is a great confidence booster for the job interview.

CHAPTER 8

THE JOB INTERVIEW

IN THIS CHAPTER

- Knowing what to expect *before* the interview
- Preparing yourself to give your best answers and ask the best questions
- Impressing your interviewers with a great follow-up
- Discovering the difference between a first interview and subsequent interviews

Finally, a phone call or letter asks you to come in for that all-important job interview. You've done your homework about the company and know the general description of the job you're interviewing for.

The hiring officer probably has set a target date to fill the position, so respond immediately.

Arranging the Interview

If the company is a local one, call and make arrangements for an interview for the next day, if possible. Also offer two other dates and times. Clear your schedule of everything else; nothing is more important than the job interview. Confirm the time and place.

If the company is out of town, phone and start off by saying you are available whenever the interviewer wants to see you. And then make yourself available at those times.

Some companies do not want to spend money to bring in a job candidate from out of town, no matter how qualified the applicant is. If you can get the firm to pay for your trip, so much the better, because then it has a financial investment in you. But if you can't, explain up front you will be happy to pay your own way. And don't bring up the subject again.

Selling Yourself

You've done your homework, so you already know about the company and job that's being offered. If you need to brush up on details, now's the time to do so before you go to the interview.

The interview is a two-way street: You want the job, and the company clearly is interested in you.

- Get to the interview at least 15 minutes early so that you have time to collect your thoughts and to examine the office setting.

- Your professional appearance, which is the first impression the hiring officer has of you, is a major factor in the decision to hire you. Wear business attire, even if you know employees generally dress casually. This is a serious, business meeting.

- Bring with you the list of references you've selected for this particular job.

- Be relaxed, friendly, and outgoing.

- Have a positive attitude and answer — and ask questions — with confidence. But don't be aggressive or brag.

- Listen carefully to the questions and take your time in answering them. Use proper grammar. Reply with full sentences, not one-word answers.

- Be yourself.

Role-play the upcoming job interview with a friend: Rehearse your answers to questions you expect to be asked. Don't forget to bring your resume and references.

Questions you'll be asked

Hiring officers are focused on finding out what your skills and experience are, if you can do the job, how you get along with other workers, if you can think quickly, and how you will fit into the corporate culture.

You may be asked questions that have nothing to do with the job just to see how flexible you are, how well you think on your feet, and how quickly you can solve a problem. Don't be taken by surprise if you're asked about your weaknesses as well as.

Some questions you'll be asked:

■ **Why did you leave your last job?** If you're looking for a better opportunity, say so. If you were forced out, say it was time to move on. No other explanations are necessary. If you go into agonizing details about why you left your last job, you won't get this one.

Never bad-mouth a former employer or colleagues, no matter how terrible they were. It's a sign of disloyalty, immaturity, and a lack of professionalism. And don't knock the job you held.

■ **What skills did you acquire in your last job that apply here?** Answer by listing your skills and accomplishments that apply to the job you're seeking, such as heading a project that pertains to the job opening.

- **Do you have the educational background to do this job?** Even if you majored in French and the job is to design software applications, explain that college taught you to think analytically and how to find answers to questions. If your education applies directly to the current job opportunity, stress how thorough it was in preparing you for your profession and this job, such as discipline you learned in the military and how the high school courses you excelled in apply.

- **How do you get along with other people?** Reassure the questioner that you are a team player and work cooperatively with others to get the job done well and on time. Add that you enjoy mentoring new hires and being mentored. And that you take directions well.

- **What are your greatest shortcomings?** It's important to give an honest answer without creating a negative impression. Present shortcomings that can be corrected with a brief training course or with minimal direction from a supervisor, such as you need to learn a new computer program or your impatience with coworkers who don't carry their share of the load.

- **Why are you interested in this company?** Here's where all the homework you've done pays off. Show your knowledge of the goals and current financial position of the firm. Explain how they appeal to you and how much you want to be part of this exciting company with such a good future.

- **What would you do if you discovered a coworker is taking bribes from a supplier?** Prove you know how businesses work by saying you would document the illegal activity in writing and immediately report it to your supervisor — but you would never consider accusing the coworker yourself or taking any direct action.

- **What do you do in your spare time?** Impress the interviewer with how well-rounded you are by describing your interests and activities — real ones. No matter how deeply involved you are in political or religious activities, do NOT mention them. They're nobody's business and could be used to rule you out of consideration for the job.

- **What's the last movie you saw?** The particular movie probably won't tell the interviewer anything about you, but if you hesitate, stammer, blush, or even freeze, it will. Smile, as if you're chatting with a friend, and give the title of the movie and when you saw it. Don't go into details unless you're asked to.

- **Why do you think you can do this job?** Sell yourself with confidence: You know you have the skills and technical know-how to do the job, or you wouldn't be called in for an interview. Cite specific achievements and professional experience that relate to the work that has to be done.

- **Are you a risk-taker?** You have to take risks in order to succeed in most jobs being created today in a fast-changing, high-tech society. Your answer is yes, you are. And give as an example of it your job search itself.

Employers are looking for candidates who communicate well, can analyze new situations, and who work well with others. They will look for proof of these attributes in your answers to their questions.

Acing written tests

Some time during the interview, possibly at the beginning of it, you may be asked to take skills, aptitude, and psychological tests. This is a fairly standard practice and you can't refuse to take them if you want to be a seriously considered. But answer them with great care, focusing on answers that show you are a good fit for the job. Be wary of questions that are overly personal or intrusive and may unfairly and, in some cases, illegally eliminate you from consideration. Don't answer them.

In most states, lie detector tests are illegal. Refuse to take one if asked.

Questions you shouldn't answer

Before an actual job offer is made, employers legally cannot ask you questions about your age, race, gender, ethnic background, religion, disability, marital status, number of children, nor your plans to have a family. Candidates are protected from answering them by federal, state, and local antidiscrimination laws. Employers who ask them are seeking discriminatory information, and most of them are aware of what they are doing.

If you are asked discriminatory questions, don't reply that you won't answer because they're illegal. That would end the interview right there. Instead, respond by saying that you will be glad to answer all personal questions when a job offer is made, particularly those pertaining to health coverage and other benefits.

Despite the fact that questions about how many children you have and family planning are both offensive and discriminatory, hiring officers ask them not to break the laws but to get a handle on your dependability and commitment to the job. Answer questions about child care, ability to travel, or other family responsibilities you may have by assuring the interviewer that you are a professional, always get your work done, have never let an employer down — and never will.

Another area to avoid talking about is what salary you expect to receive. Just as you omitted any mention of wages on your resume, try not to discuss money during the first interview: You might be disqualifying yourself from consideration. If asked specifically about salary expectations or what you made previously, answer vaguely. Give a wide salary range, such as "in the $30,000s." Or, if you know the company's range for this job category, state a figure in the middle.

When you did your homework, you learned what salary the job should pay. Save that information for negotiating your pay and benefits package. But meanwhile, the interviewer needs reassurance that the company's not wasting its time with you, that you are agreeable to their salary range. Ask specifically what they are thinking of paying and use the information to determine how to negotiate for what you want.

When questions about salary arise, state that you want the job very much and that you are certain that your compensation will not be a problem.

Asking the Right Questions

There's additional information you will need about the job opening and it's important for you to ask questions: You need to know the answers and the interviewer will evaluate you positively for wanting to know more about the job. Prepare your questions.

Business-related questions

Questions you should consider asking include

■ What opportunities are there for me to advance in my department and in the company?

- What kind of training do you give? How do you develop employees?

- To whom do I report?

- How often do you give performance appraisals?

- Do you have an orientation program for new employees?

- How large is my department?

- Is the company planning to expand or cut back?

- How much travel is involved?

- Do you emphasize teamwork?

- Is the work usually done on a project-to-project basis?

Remember

You will be working for most of your life, and job satisfaction is an important element in achieving the quality of life you want. Now is the time to ask questions that do not directly pertain to your job performance or career outlook, but which have bearing on your future lifestyle.

Work life versus personal life questions

The No. 1 concern of employees is the ability to balance their work lives with their personal lives — whether or not they are married and have children. Having flexibility and company support to achieve it will make a major difference in your personal and job satisfaction, so ask the necessary questions to find out the employer's commitment to these issues.

- How much vacation time do you give after what period of time?

- Do you offer flexible work arrangements?

- Do you have a child care center or a child care referral service?

- When employees have to travel overnight or business, do you help them secure or pay for child care?

- How much overtime is necessary to get the job done?

Standing out in a Crowd

Even though there are several other applicants for the job, you are the most qualified and enthusiastic — and you want to make sure that the interviewer knows that. You can do several things to make sure that he does.

How to end the interview

When you are asked for your list of references, you will know that this first session is drawing to a close. Use the remaining time to stress once again your flexibility about assignments, how well you work with teams, and your desire to mentor others. Cite projects you've worked on in previous jobs and emphasize how thoroughly you did them and that you completed them on time.

Let the hiring officer end the interviewer, not you. Smile, shake hands, repeat how much you'd like to work for the company, and say thank you for the time.

Don't be shy about asking when you can expect to hear from the company and if the interviewer thinks you are the right fit for the job in question. The answers will give you some indication about how the interview went and what your chances are. Say you hope to be back very soon.

Don't forget to write a thank you

After the interview, write a thank you note to the hiring officer. You can refer to the sample letter in Figure 8-1 to get you started. Your letter will serve the purpose of showing you're a professional and of reminding them how eager you are to work for them. Write it on the same letterhead you used for your cover letter.

Warn your references

Notify your references that you have given their names and phone numbers and to expect a phone call. Go over with them what you want emphasized. Ask them to let you know when they are called and what they said.

That All-Important Second Interview (and Third, and Fourth . . .)

Most companies do not make a job offer after only one interview.

You have to prepare carefully to do well in the second job interview, too. And the third. And fourth.

Getting a second interview

The second interview usually comes within two weeks of the first one. If you haven't heard from the person you interviewed with within one week of sending your thank you letter, call and try to arrange a second interview.

Figure 8-1: Sample thank you letter.

Jane Doe
300 E. Elm St.
Chicago, IL 60611
312-777-8001
janedoe@aol.com

(Today's Date)

John Smith
Executive Vice President, Marketing
XYZ Food Brands, Inc.
6000 W. Wacker Drive
Chicago, IL 60004

Dear Mr. Smith,

Thank you so much for interviewing me for the job of marketing director for your company. I hope I answered all your questions and that I fit your needs. As you now know, I am excited about your marketing plans and want to be a part of them.

I am available for a follow-up interview at any time and will call you next week to ascertain your interest in my candidacy — unless I hear from you first. As you can tell, I'm very interested in working for your excellent firm. Thanks again for your consideration of me.

Sincerely,

Jane Doe

Though you will feel more relaxed during the second and subsequent interviews, remember that they are as serious as the first one.

At the second meeting, once again wear business attire, unless you've learned from your first visit that informality truly is the rule. Be prepared to be interviewed by someone different. And once again, bring along your list of references.

Changing your focus

In follow-up interviews, instead of again assessing your experience and professional skills, most employers focus on finding out if you're willing to learn the new job, have a strong work ethic, and are the best match for the job to be done. They look for flexibility, a positive attitude, and for any signs that you may not be a good fit with the organization. They want to evaluate your skills, behavior, and general character in context of the company's stated values.

You may be given a hypothetical, extremely tough job-related problem to solve. Prepare for that possibility: You will not be judged for the speed with which you come up with your solutions but for what they are, how you present them, and the insights they give into your grasp of the responsibilities you might have to handle and the corporate culture.

Fitting in with the company culture

In the second interview, the hiring officer will try to ascertain how well you will fit in with the company culture. Expect questions about your personal ethics, loyalty to your employer, how much training you will need, your attitude toward gossip and office romances, your availability during crunch times, and getting your work done without prodding from management.

You may be introduced to other officers at the company and interviewed by each of them: Don't be nervous about this; it's a sign of interest in you and the company's desire for feedback from other people.

Following up

A phone call to the hiring officers rather than a letter of thanks is appropriate after the second and subsequent interviews. Once again, notify your references. Be optimistic about an employment offer, but don't give up your job search yet.

CHAPTER 9

NAILING THE JOB

IN THIS CHAPTER

- Researching your job offer
- Negotiating your best deal
- Accepting the job

You clearly know the company is interested in you and you're eagerly awaiting an offer — while continuing your job search.

Often companies, particularly large ones, do not immediately fill the job opening. They might want to interview several other candidates; they might decide not to hire anyone for a few months or longer; they may even decide not to fill the position.

Keeping in Touch

To find out where you stand in the hiring process, you need to keep in touch with your contacts at the company.

- Call the hiring officer at least once a week. Ask whether it's okay to call every week and try to find out what the timetable is for filling the job.

- Call your networking contacts inside the firm at least once a week. Invite them to lunch. Ask them what they know about the status of the job being filled and your prospects.

- Keep abreast of any new developments or changes at the company.

The Job Offer

Finally, you get a job offer, either by phone or in a letter. Answer immediately by telephone. You can expect to be asked during the phone call whether you plan to accept. If you know you want the job, it's okay to say yes. But it's much wiser not to say yes immediately. Instead, hold off blindly accepting and instead say how excited and happy you are and that you will discuss all details at the next meeting.

When you make arrangements for the meeting, ask whom it will be with. Get the correct name, title, location, and phone number. When you actually negotiate for a job, it's often with someone other than the person who originally screened you.

Doing your salary homework

- Before you go to the negotiating meeting, ask whether the company has salary grades, what yours is, and what the range is. You want your pay to be at least in the middle of the salary range for your job.

- Call your regional office of the U.S. Bureau of Labor Statistics for information on starting and average salaries in your field.

- Check with professional associations to find out what members in similar positions earn.

- Ask friends and colleagues in your field what they are paid. If they're reluctant to tell you, ask for a salary range or advice as to what you should ask for.

- Talk to executive recruiters about pay levels for candidates they place in your field.

- Do an Internet search of wages in your profession. Go to a chat room and ask for salary information — but remember, it may not be reliable and you don't know where it's coming from.

- Also find out from each of these sources what the typical benefits and perks are for your job.

Discussing the salary with confidence

After the job offer is made — and before you actually accept — you have considerable leverage and bargaining power. Use them to your advantage, but don't come on too strong or aggressively: You don't want to turn off the interviewer — and lose the job opportunity.

Act as if both you and the hiring officer are equals, discussing an important subject: Money.

Negotiating your salary

You don't want to enter salary negotiations without being prepared. Keep the following tips in mind when you negotiate your salary:

- Based on your knowledge of the salary range, establish a minimum amount that you won't go below. Stick to it. The employer will be impressed with your knowledge of pay — and that you know what you want and what you should get. This will influence the offer because it will be clear you are confident about what you should be paid for your abilities.

- If you don't like the initial offer, say so and give your reasons.

- Keep negotiating for more.

- If you're not getting anywhere and salary is important to you, say so. At that point, you might decide not to take the job.

- If you still want the job and the company isn't budging from its proposal, suggest a one-time cash bonus for accepting the offer. Most companies don't tell you that they offer a hiring bonus — even though most of them will give them to deserving new hires — so don't hesitate to ask for one. It should be at least 10 percent of the annual salary offered.

■ If you're switching jobs, it's reasonable to expect an increase in salary. Most employers understand this. If the offer is less than or the same as what you were previously making, remind your employer of this. If it's still too low and you feel you're at an impasse but want the job, then the down-and-dirty negotiations should begin.

Ways to increase your offer

If a company has budgeted a certain amount of money for an annual salary, your starting wage probably is written in stone. If the salary isn't as high as you had hoped, you can still improve the value of your pay package.

Tip

Here's what to ask for:

■ A different title, one that will put you in a better salary grade. Suggest a specific title.

■ A salary review within six months.

■ Special perks such as a car, car allowance, free parking, more vacation days, paid attendance at seminars, paid club memberships, paid subscriptions to publications in your field, and paid membership in professional associations.

■ Agree to accept the salary offered for extra stock options, especially if it's a start-up company.

Commissions and incentive pay are cash awards that are popular with employers because they're based on performance. Find out what they're awarded for and if you will receive one

Negotiating benefits

Though benefits aren't cash, they can be worth thousands of dollars to you annually, particularly if you receive health insurance. Here are the benefits you should get or request:

- Medical, dental, life, and disability insurance
- Profit sharing
- Retirement plan and 401(k) benefits
- Paid vacation
- Tuition refund
- Child and elder care allowance or subsidy
- Flexible hours
- Telecommuting options
- Paid sick leave — how many days?
- Paid or subsidized membership in a health club or sports facility
- If you have to relocate, ask for the full amount of the cost of relocations — paid airfare for you and your family, automobile mileage, help in selling your present home and buying a new one, living costs while relocating, and assisting your spouse in finding a job and locating child care. If the company only offers a lump sum for relocation, make sure that it covers your expenses.

Most people judge their success on how much money they earn — and are judged that way by others. Make sure that you're comfortable with the value of your final package.

Special considerations

If you're a woman or minority, make sure that sufficient numbers of other women and minorities are employed or are managers — an indication of the company's commitment to diversity and to your own personal advancement.

Accepting the Job Offer

If the new job meets most of your personal and professional requirements, accept the offer. But if you're still not certain, ask for time to think it over. Tell the employer you will call them in 24 hours with your decision (or the following Monday, if the offer was made on a Friday).

Get it in writing

After accepting the offer, ask for the details in writing, including your responsibilities, salary and bonus, benefits, to whom you report, and your start date. If the company won't give you written documentation — which makes it legally binding — you should put the terms of the agreement in a letter to the hiring officer and keep a copy for yourself. The sample agreement in Figure 9-1 gives you some tips.

Verbal agreements also are binding — but are harder to prove.

Signing contracts

Some companies, wary of turnover, ask new employees to sign a contract stating that they will not leave to work for a competitor within a certain time frame, usually from three to five years. And because the cost of training is so high, some firms also ask you to sign a contract to pay back costs of your training if you quit within a specified amount of time. Most new hires don't like to sign these agreements, but you probably won't get the job unless you do.

Congratulations! You've gotten the job you want.

Figure 9-1: Sample letter of agreement.

Use the date of your acceptance of the job offer as the date for your letter and address it to the hiring officer you negotiated with.

Dear Ms. Jones:

I am extremely pleased to accept your offer for the job of marketing manager at your excellent company. I'm looking forward to starting on Monday, October 10.

According to our discussions, I will be in charge of the marketing for all brands the company handles and will report to James Jones, executive vice president of marketing. I will have a staff of 20 people and the authority to hire and fire, at my own discretion, the employees who report to me.

My starting salary will be $85,000 a year with a hiring bonus of $8,500. I will receive the bonus on the day I start. I will receive annual raises and can also expect an annual, year-end bonus, both based on my performance.

We have agreed that I will have three weeks vacation my first year on the job and four weeks after that time. I will have six days of paid sick leave and will be allowed to telecommute from my home one day a week. And, of course, as an executive, I will put in whatever overtime is necessary, without extra pay, to get the job done.

Additionally, my hiring package includes stock options, a retirement plan, medical coverage, and life and disability insurance. I will also be given paid membership in the National Association of Marketing Professionals and subscriptions to daily newspapers and professional organizations. I will provide my own car, but my car expenses will be paid for by the company and I will have free parking on the premises. I will also have an expense account so that I can be reimbursed for business-related activities.

And, my family is delighted that you also offered me a paid family membership at a local health club!

This letter represents my employment and compensation package as I understand it. If there are any changes or additions, please let me know as soon as possible.

Once again, I am excited about your job offer and about being part of such an outstanding organization.

Sincerely,

Jane Doe

CHAPTER 10

LIFE AFTER THE JOB

IN THIS CHAPTER

- Deciding how and when to give notice
- Remembering the importance of behaving professionally

You have the job you want, but if you're also still working for someone else, with money coming in and the protection of benefits, you still have a job to do. You've positioned yourself well up to this point for the last few days with your current employer by acting professionally, by keeping your job search a secret, and being up to date on all of your work responsibilities.

Giving Notice

When you've agreed on a starting date with your new employer, give at least two weeks notice to your present employer. Tell your current manager first; after that, you can tell colleagues. If you notify your boss in writing, keep it simple: Just state the name of your new employer and when you will leave. Don't give any reason for leaving; it's not necessary. It's also wise to add a line saying how much you enjoyed working there — even if you didn't.

Though it may be very flattering that your new boss wants you to start immediately, don't do it — unless you're told to leave right away by your present employer. Your new employer will respect you for your professional commitment. Instead, finish up as many projects as you can, offer to help find and train a replacement, and, if possible, take some time for yourself to recover from your intensive job search and to prepare for the new one.

Don't be surprised if after you give notice your current employer says today is your last day. Many companies consider it demoralizing to the rest of the staff that an employee has found a new — and perhaps better — job. Another concern is security. Continue to act professionally.

Leaving immediately

If you're asked to leave immediately:

- Make an appointment to meet with the human resource department to iron out your exit details.

- Pack up all your possessions. Don't forget anything because in all likelihood you won't be allowed back in your department.

- From home, call the former colleagues you want to say goodbye to, but don't make any negative comments about your former — and their present — employer.

Staying on

If it's a tight labor market, your employer may make a counteroffer to try to induce you to stay on. A counteroffer usually includes more money, more perks, and possibly a promotion.

I often have observed that the counteroffer isn't as flattering as it first seems. It too often is the company's way of taking control of your leaving, to keep you on board until someone else can be found to take your place. And then you're gone — at the company's convenience. That's why I advise politely yet firmly turning down the counteroffer, no matter how generous it seems.

Getting through the Last Two Weeks

Try to finish up everything on your desk, especially your share of team projects, and if you do have a replacement, focus on giving her the best training you can. Your aim is to work hard up until the last minute in your present job and to make sure that everyone thinks well of you after you've gone.

If you didn't use your present employer as a reference for fear of losing your job, be aware that your new employer, even though the job offer has been made and accepted, still might contact your supervisor for more information about you. You want to get the glowing reference you deserve.

If you've been fired or downsized, request a written reference to take with you to give to your new employer. Having a letter in hand that the writer knows you will see is better than risking a telephone conversation between your present and future employer that might hurt your prospects.

Handling the exit interview

Many companies have exit interviews, and you have to go through them in order to sign off from your present job. Be prepared for the process to test your self-control and professionalism.

No matter how angry or frustrated you are in your present job, don't vent your feelings at the exit interview.

The company will want to know what you think is wrong with your manager and colleagues, perhaps to correct any problems and to improve your replacement's performance. Though it's flattering to be asked your opinion, it's not your responsibility to enlighten your employers or to help them manage better. As in a job interview, speak no evil and merely say that you are leaving because it was time to move on, that you have no quarrel with the way your department is being run — and little else.

Cleaning up the odds and ends

Severing financial arrangements can be complicated. You might first want to talk to an accountant or employment lawyer regarding your options and the transfer of funds.

Be sure to ask about how to handle such matters as your retirement pension or 401(k) plan, vacation and sick days that are due you, medical and life insurance plans, lump sum payments, deferred bonuses, and profit-sharing plan.

If you've been fired or laid off, figure out exactly what your severance pay, which usually is one week's pay for each year you've worked there, should be.

Much of the money you will receive from various company plans will be taxable — unless you roll it into an IRA.

Hitting the Ground Running

The day you start your new job is a much anticipated and exciting one. It also sets the pattern of what your day to day life will be like in your new position.

Be in charge of your new career from Day One. It's up to you to make it move forward by managing yourself.

Organizing your work life

No one expects you to do a perfect job — or even much work at all — your first day, but you do have to show you meet your responsibilities, are a team player, and fit in with the company culture. Use your first days and weeks to get to know colleagues, team members, bosses — and how things work.

Ask a lot of questions but only of people who have time to answer.

Acing your first day

Follow these tips to set the correct tone on your first day.

- Arrive early and leave a few minutes late.

- Make an appointment with your manager to find out all the details of the job. The meeting might not be possible on your first day, particularly if it's a Monday, but make sure that you have one within a few days.

- If no one takes you around to introduce you to the staff, be proactive and introduce yourself.

- Try to meet everyone on your team. Find out what their individual responsibilities are and where you fit in.

- If no one asks you to go to lunch, ask someone yourself.

- Don't be nervous — and if you are, try not to show it.

If you don't have a mentor, get one — or several of them. As a new hire, you want to know what the boss is really like, the real chain of command, who are the movers and shakers, what the new projects will be, and what training programs are being offered.

Don't be shy about asking for the help you need. Your colleagues probably will be extremely cooperative, especially in a team setting where the success of everyone depends on each individual's accomplishments. Sit down and organize your work on a daily or weekly basis — and don't overschedule yourself.

If your new company has an employee handbook, read it carefully and understand that the rules are to be taken seriously and obeyed. Companies issue handbooks (which are often written by lawyers) to employees to establish regulations that protect the company.

It's okay to ask immediately about training you'll receive to learn how to do your job, starting with how to use your computer.

At the end of six months, ask your manager how you're doing. If your starting salary wasn't satisfactory to you, ask for a meeting to discuss a raise.

CLIFFSNOTES REVIEW

Use this CliffsNotes Review to practice what you've learned in this book and to build your confidence in doing the job right the first time. After you work through the review questions, the problem-solving exercises, and the fun and useful practice projects, you're well on your way to achieving your goal of getting a job.

Q&A

1. The three different types of resumes are

_____

_____

_____

2. There are several ways to send your resume to potential employers. List three:

_____

_____

_____

3. Which of the following questions should you *not* answer during an interview?

a. What is your favorite movie?

b. If you suspected a coworker was embezzling money from the company, what would you do?

c. Are you willing to work on Sundays even though it may hinder you from attending church?

d. Do you have a college education?

4. Which of the following are benefits and perks besides salary that you can negotiate to ensure that you get the deal you want?

a. Fitness reimbursement

b. Flexible hours

c. Relocation expenses

d. Extra stock options

e. All of the above

Answers: (1) Chronological, skills or functional, and historical or anecdotal. (2) Regular mail or courier, in the body of an e-mail letter, as an e-mail attachment (provided the recipient knows it's coming and thus trusts it won't be infected by a virus), by filling out a form on the company's Web site, or hand delivery. (3) c. (4) e.

Scenario

1. You accepted a job offer, gave at least two weeks notice to your current employer, and will participate in an exit interview before you leave. Your friends think it's a great opportunity to explain how unfair and overly demanding your manager was to work for, but instead you should _____.

Answers: (1) Be very gracious and speak in nonspecific, general terms. Never talk badly about anyone in the organization because you never know if you'll come across them again in your professional life.

Consider This

■ Did you know that millions of jobs are advertised on the Internet? You can browse the careers sites, talk with other job seekers in chat rooms, and even have new ads e-mailed to you on a regular basis. Turn to Chapter 4 for more information on using the Internet in your job search.

■ Did you know technology jobs such as Web page designer and computer programmer are among the fastest growing careers for the next ten years? Read Chapter 2 to find out which jobs and industries are hot and which are fading away.

Practice Project

1. Talk to people you admire in your field. Ask them what they think are good job-hunting strategies. Join a professional organization and get involved — you may find a mentor who can guide you to your next job and beyond! See Chapter 4 to find out more about this.

2. Write down your five-year plans for both your professional and personal life. Are your goals realistic? Do you have a clear strategy to meet them? See Chapter 1 for more information.

3. Create a sample referral letter for your references detailing the important information they need to have at their fingertips when they are approached by prospective employers. Turn to Chapter 7 for more information on references.

4. Ask a friend to role-play your job interview with you. Write a series of questions you think the interviewer will ask you and have your friend ask you those questions until you feel confident and comfortable with your answers. Ask that person for critical feedback on your performance. Check out Chapter 8 for more advice on preparing for a job interview.

CLIFFSNOTES RESOURCE CENTER

The learning doesn't need to stop here. CliffsNotes Resource Center shows you the best of the best — links to the best information in print and online about getting a job. And don't think that this is all we've prepared for you; we've put all kinds of pertinent information at www.cliffsnotes.com. Look for all the terrific resources at your favorite bookstore or local library and on the Internet. When you're online, make your first stop www.cliffsnotes.com where you'll find more incredibly useful information about getting a job.

Books

This CliffsNotes book is one of many great books about getting a job published by IDG Books Worldwide, Inc. So if you want some great next-step books, check out these other publications:

Job Hunting For Dummies, by Max Messmer, arms you with additional skills and tools for landing a job. IDG Books Worldwide, Inc. $16.99

Resumes For Dummies, 2nd Edition, by Joyce Lain Kennedy, gives you more step-by-step guidelines for creating a smashing resume. IDG Books Worldwide, Inc. $12.99.

Cover Letters For Dummies, by Joyce Lain Kennedy, gives you more detail on creating cover letters with impact. IDG Books Worldwide, Inc. $12.99.

Job Interviews For Dummies, by Joyce Lain Kennedy, tells you everything you need to know about conducting a "Show-Stopper" interview. IDG Books Worldwide, Inc. $12.99.

Cool Careers For Dummies, by Marty Nemko and Paul and Sarah Edwards, gives you the scoop on more than 500 great careers. IDG Books Worldwide, Inc. $16.99.

It's easy to find books published by IDG Books Worldwide, Inc. You'll find them in your favorite bookstores (on the Internet and at a store near you). We also have three Web sites that you can use to read about all the books we publish:

- www.cliffsnotes.com
- www.dummies.com
- www.idgbooks.com

Internet

Check out these Web sites for more information about getting a job and more:

America's Job Bank, www.ajb.dni.us, maintained by the U.S. Department of Labor and coordinated by the 50 state employment services, is updated daily and has an average listing of half a million jobs.

National Board for Certified Counselors (NACC), www.nbcc.org, will send you a list of certified career counselors in your area.

National Career Development Association (NCDA), www.ncda.org, will connect you with counselors in your area.

International Association of Career Management Professionals, www.iacmp.org, hooks you up with its members, who are mostly career development and outplacement professionals.

Society for Human Resource Management (SHRM), www.shrm.org/hrlinks, gives you information on topics such as general resources, compensation and benefits, and education and training.

Next time you're on the Internet, don't forget to drop by www.cliffsnotes.com. We created an online Resource Center that you can use today, tomorrow, and beyond.

Send Us Your Favorite Tips

In your quest for learning, have you ever experienced that sublime moment when you figure out a trick that saves time or trouble? Perhaps you realized you were taking ten steps to accomplish something that could have taken two. Or you found a little-known workaround that gets great results. If you've discovered a useful tip that helped you get a job more effectively and you'd like to share it, the CliffsNotes staff would love to hear from you. Go to our Web site at www.cliffsnotes.com and click the Talk to Us button. If we select your tip, we may publish it as part of CliffsNotes Daily, our exciting, free e-mail newsletter. To find out more or to subscribe to a newsletter, go to www.cliffsnotes.com on the Web.

INDEX

A

agricultural job growth, 28
America's Job Bank, 37, 43
antidiscrimination laws, 54, 90

B

benefits, negotiating, 102
business job growth, 21
business publications, 39

C

career marketers, 11, 13
CareerPath, 43
changing careers, 13–15
choosing careers
  counseling, 10–13
  evaluating personal needs, 6–8
  identifying growth fields, 19–23, 27
  identifying non-growth fields, 28–29
  investigating jobs , 29–32
  matching preferences to jobs, 16–18
classified ads, 42
CliffsNotes Web site, 3
college resources, 45
communication skills, 15
company research. See researching
  employers
conferences, 46
construction job growth, 28
contracts, 103
corporate culture, 16, 74, 87, 96
counseling, 10, 12–13
cover letters
  addressee, 67, 73
  dating, 73
  e-mailing, 75
  faxing, 74
  hand delivering, 74
  length, 68
  mailing, 74
  role, 65–66
  special situations, 69, 73
  stationery, 68

topics to avoid, 67
writing, 67–68

D

discrimination, 54, 90
dress, 86

E

education job growth, 22
e-mailing resumes, 75
employers, researching. See researching
  employers
employment agencies, 50–51
employment gaps, 55, 62
engineering field growth, 22
entertainment job growth, 23
expenses
  counseling, 10, 12
  employment agencies, 51
  joining professional organizations, 45
  travel, 86

F

financial services job growth, 21
five-year plan, 8–10
following up
  job offers, 99, 103
  leads, 49
  references, 84
  resume receipt, 74, 76
  second interviews, 97
  thank you letters, 93, 95

G

goals
  five-year plan, 8–10
  realistic expectations, 8
  self assessment, 7–8
government job growth, 22
growth fields, 19–23, 27

H

headhunters, 49–50
hiring bonuses, 100
hospitality job growth, 22

I

information technology job growth, 21
informational interviews, 29
International Association of Career
    Management Professionals, 115
Internet resources
  America's Job Bank, 37, 43
  CareerPath, 43
  CliffsNotes Web site, 3
  company research, 36–38
  International Association of Career
    Management Professionals, 115
  job search component, 43–45
  Monster, 43
  National Board for Certified
    Counselors (NACC), 115
  National Career Development
    Association (NCDA), 115
  resume posting, 76
  Society for Human Resource
    Management (SHRM), 116
internships, 31
interviews. *See also* informational
    interviews
  arranging, 85
  dress, 86
  ending, 93
  questions asked, 87–89
  questions disallowed, 90
  questions to ask, 91–92
  salary discussion, 90–91
  second interviews, 94, 96–97
  thank you letter, 93, 95
  travel expenses, 86

J

job banks, 46
job clubs, 47–48
job fairs, 48–49
job interviews. *See* interviews
job offers
  follow-up, 99
  hiring bonus, 100
  letters of agreement, 103, 104
  negotiating benefits, 102
  negotiating salary, 100–101
  perks, 101
  refusing, 100

job research
  identifying growing fields, 19–23
  identifying non-growth fields, 28–29
  internships, 31
  interviewing, 29
  questions to ask, 34–35
  salary, 99–100
  shadowing, 30
  volunteering, 31
job search
  classified ads, 42
  college resources, 45
  employment agencies, 50–51
  headhunters, 49–50
  Internet resources, 43–45
  job banks, 46
  job clubs, 47–48
  job fairs, 48–49
  meetings and conferences, 46
  networking, 52
  part-time work, 50–51
  pre-search homework, 34–40
  professional organizations, 45–46
  telephoning, 42–43
  temporary service agencies, 50–51
job shadowing, 30

L

lawsuits, 83
letters of recommendation, 82
library resources, 38, 39
lie detector tests, 90
lying, 83

M

manufacturing job growth, 28
marketers, 11, 13
media job growth, 23
media resources, 40
meetings (professional conferences), 46
mining job growth, 28
Monster, 43
Myers-Briggs Type Indicator test, 10

N

National Board for Certified Counselors (NACC), 12, 115
National Career Development Association (NCDA), 115
networking, 40, 52
newspaper resources, 39
non-growth fields, 28–29

O

objectives. *See* goals
Occupational Outlook Handbook, 21
offers of employment. *See* job offers
outplacement services, 12

P

part-time work, 50
personal characteristics
    employer wish list, 14–15
    matching to jobs, 16–18, 34–35
    testing, 10
personal services field, 23
placement centers, 11–12
planning, 8–10
professional organizations, 45–46

R

references
    bad references, 83
    bringing to interview, 86
    follow-up calls, 84
    format, 79
    letters of recommendation, 82
    notifying, 80, 94
    occasion to supply, 79
    recruiting, 78–83
refusing jobs, 100
relocation costs, 102
researching employers
    Internet resources, 36–38, 45
    library resources, 38–39
    media resources, 40
    newspaper resources, 39
    planning your search, 35
    questions to ask, 34
resumes. *See also* cover letters
    baseline resumes, 53
    brevity, 54

chronological resumes, 57, 59, 68, 70
    dating, 73
    e-mailing, 75
    employer databases, 73, 75
    employment gaps, 55, 62
    essential components, 57
    faxing, 74
    follow-up, 74
    formatting, 75
    hand delivering, 74
    historical resumes, 60, 62–64, 68, 72
    Internet posting, 76
    keywords, 73
    length, 56
    mailing, 74
    personal information, 54
    photos, 54
    salary, 55–56
    skills resumes, 57–58, 61, 68, 71
    topics to avoid, 54–55
    volunteer work, 55

S

salary
    discussion at interviews, 90–91
    negotiating, 100–101
    researching, 99–100
    resumes, 55–56
    switching careers, 13
sales job growth, 23
science job growth, 23
self evaluation
    goals, 7–8
    psychological testing, 10
    situation, 6–8
skills
    matching to jobs, 16–18
    transferable skills, 13
social services job growth, 22
Society for Human Resource Management (SHRM), 116
stationery, 68
switching careers, 13–15

T

telephoning
    follow-up calls, 49, 74
    initial contact, 42–43
    interview follow-up, 98
    networking, 52

temporary service agencies, 50–51
thank you letters, 93, 95
transferable skills, 13
travel expenses, 86

U

university resources, 45

V

volunteer work, 31, 55

W

written tests, 89

CliffsNotes™

Your shortcut to
success™
for over 40 years

Computers and Software
Confused by computers? Struggling with software? Let
CliffsNotes get you up to speed on the fundamentals —
quickly and easily. Titles include:

Balancing Your Checkbook with Quicken®
Buying Your First PC
Creating a Dynamite PowerPoint® 2000 Presentation
Making Windows® 98 Work for You
Setting up a Windows® 98 Home Network
Upgrading and Repairing Your PC
Using Your First PC
Using Your First iMac™
Writing Your First Computer Program

The Internet
Intrigued by the Internet? Puzzled about life online?
Let *CliffsNotes* show you how to get started with e-mail,
Web surfing, and more. Titles include:

Buying and Selling on eBay®
Creating Web Pages with HTML
Creating Your First Web Page
Exploring the Internet with Yahoo!®
Finding a Job on the Web
Getting on the Internet
Going Online with AOL®
Shopping Online Safely